The Basic Arts of Budgeting

THE BASIC ARTS
OF BUDGETING

T. S. McAlpine, ACCA, ACMA

BUSINESS BOOKS LIMITED
London

First published 1976

ISBN 0 220 66269 x

*This book has been set 11 on 12 point Baskerville
and prepared for press by The Ivory Head Press,
170 Murray Road, London W5, and printed in England by
W & J Mackay Limited, Chatham
for the publishers, Business Books Limited,
24 Highbury Crescent, London N5*

Contents

Preface

The increasing complexity of business operations and the ever-changing conditions of the business environment — social, economic, technological and political developments — make it increasingly difficult for a company to consistently earn a profit that constitutes a fair return on the capital investment. Management has to have a plan of action as a means of protecting profit. Planning cannot, of course, guarantee profit in all circumstances, but it can provide safeguards.

In a changing environment companies have to make changes to keep up to date. These changes may await events or anticipate them. Anticipating and preparing for change simply underlines the basic need for forward planning; determining the aims and objectives of the business in the light of probable events and making plans and programmes for achieving them.

There are many examples of progressive companies, some of international repute, that have founded their success on efficient planning and effective implementation. The question, therefore, is not whether planning is essential but how it should be orientated to meet the particular requirements of the individual business.

In the majority of companies, planning, and not least profit planning and control through budgeting procedures, still remains an underdeveloped function and there is con-

siderable scope for applying it more extensively and more
efficiently. Planning in one form or another is present in every
business but too often this tends to be partial rather than
comprehensive, spasmodic instead of systematic, based on in-
sufficient information and facts and not done with the object
of allocating responsibilities and monitoring performance.
There also remains a hard core of inherently capable executives who are still prepared to navigate a business through *ad
hoc* decisions on matters of major importance — recognised as
a virtue perhaps, two or three decades ago but which inevitably place a business at risk in the present conditions.

There is a large body of knowledge associated with
management which should be known to managers. Management efficiency stems from knowledge, understanding, application and learning. There is a wide gap between the
average knowledge and performance of management and that
of the leaders yet all the information and guidelines are
available to raise the general standards of management performance. Every manager should appreciate and understand
the principles and practices that make a business tick. As the
chairman of a large European complex expressed it 'today's
manager has to be everything from a sociologist to a cost
analyst'.

Sophisticated management is the key to better planning
and better performance.

The primary purpose of budgeting is profit planning and
control and in this connection it is concerned with every
aspect and every activity of a business. The essence of accurate
budgeting is to be close to the events and for this reason it is
unusual to operate through an annual budget as the ideal
period. There is the further aspect that the performance of
companies is judged by the annual accounts and it follows
that management should focus its profit aims on the same
period.

There are two distinct stages in budgeting: first there is
the formulation of the plans and the means of achieving them,
and second the translation of these plans into financial terms
and preparing a profit budget and balance sheet. The first
stage is generally a function of line management and the
second an accounting function.

The title of this book is *The Basic Arts of Budgeting*.
What constitutes the art of budgeting?

The art of budgeting can best be summed up by a statement made by a group of European experts who visited many
American companies selected for their good managerial
practices:

'Forecasts and estimates are not new to the business
world . . . . What is original in America is the precision
of the methods used, the budgets being drawn up on the
basis of a meticulous and systematic analysis of the
component industrial and commercial operations. Few
European companies draw up budgets in this meticulous
way or use them as an instrument of management
control'.

How management views its function and its responsibilities is probably the most influential factor in budgeting.
Business planning has to be motivated, directed, coordinated
and controlled through the personal involvement of top
management to be fully effective.

Forecasting and estimating are elements of budgeting
but these must be applied systematically and factually to
ensure that in the final analysis budgets are statements of
probability. As the chief executive of a large and highly
successful company has stated 'We go to great lengths to
establish the facts'. Budgets that project probabilities provide
a positive basis for management to determine a plan of action
for achieving its expectations. They also provide a sound basis
for allocating individual responsibility and accountability for
performance.

Books on budgeting are generally written for accountants
and students of accounting and therefore tend to concentrate
on what has been described above as the second stage of
budgeting, i.e. the translation of the plans into financial terms
and preparation of a profit budget and balance sheet, which
is the accounting function.

The present book is aimed at management and persons
associated with the planning and the implementation of the
plans. Since plans can only materialise into budgets when
expressed in financial terms the accounting function is described comprehensively.

As stated the aim is to consider budgeting in all its aspects in relation to the total operations of a business and the factors that can have a major impact on its performance. It stresses the need for management to have a sound knowledge and understanding of the business and how it operates as a pre-requisite to effective planning and outlines some of the considerations involved. The factual approach to decision-making is emphasised and as a corollary to this the management of essential information is discussed.

The more important factors fundamental to the success of a business are described. The entrepreneurial activities of a business — products, markets, volume of sales and related profit — have been considered. The need for a company to see its sales volume in terms of products and markets for the next two or three years as a means of protecting its sales income is discussed. This projection is obviously outside the scope of an annual budget and this leads to a consideration of the total planning requirements of a business.

The total planning requirements, generally termed corporate planning, are described in detail under the headings of strategic planning, long-term budgeting, operational planning and control and profit planning through annual budgeting.

Although this book is written primarily for managers it is hoped that it may prove useful to students of management, accounting and business studies.

1 An Outline of Business Planning

The increasing complexity of business and the ever-changing conditions of the business environment — social, economic, technological and political changes — make it increasingly difficult for a company to consistently earn a profit that constitutes a fair return on the capital investment. Management has to have a plan of action for the business if profits are to be protected.

In general there is no lack of planning in business, especially planning that is directed at influencing the end results of the financial year when management performance will be judged on the profit earned. For a variety of reasons, much of this planning can be ineffective; for example, it may be misdirected, or be based on opinions and generalisations instead of a fact-founded approach; it may be uncoordinated or it may fail to allocate responsibility and accountability for performance. Better planning is one of the frontiers of better management.

Planning should start by deciding and defining the objectives of the company, making sure in the process that these are compatible with the skills and resources of the undertaking. This is no simple task and until a company acquires experience in formalised planning the objectives may be vague and indeterminate and any planning based on them could be misdirected.

Opinions and generalisations are the antithesis of effective planning. Management is not fulfilling its function if it is prepared to decide as a matter of opinion what can be established as a matter of fact. Coordination in companies is difficult and the best means of ensuring it is through a proper planning procedure that demonstrates and communicates the interdependence of people, departments and functions in achieving the common objective.

Planning procedures can never be fully effective unless these are linked with responsibility and accountability for performance. This applies to top management level and throughout the whole of the organisation.

Management can only function properly and efficiently if it accepts the need for a planning discipline that will anticipate and evaluate changes and ensure that the company is prepared for them.

1.1   Budgeting

The paramount consideration in business is profit; without it there can be no business. The essential discipline is profit planning and control and this requires the application of a budgeting procedure.

Budgeting has long been recognised as the accepted procedure for profit planning and many of the most successful companies have applied it to good effect over a period of years. Some companies attach so much importance to it that it is regarded as a factor of efficient management and not simply a procedure.

Budgeting is obtaining wider acceptance but it could be applied more extensively and more effectively. Despite its obvious advantages to a company, budgeting still remains an under-developed practice.

The period generally adopted for budgeting is one year and this usually coincides with the financial year of the company. There are at least two good reasons for an annual budget. The performance of management is judged by the profit earned in the financial year and an annual budget enables management to focus its attention and efforts on all the factors that can influence sales and profit. The essence of budgeting is to be close to the events and a year is generally considered to be the ideal period. Some companies budget three to five years ahead but as the period is lengthened the reliability of the budget will be impaired. Extensions of the annual budget have their uses as a means of presenting figures that are intended to be indicative rather than strictly accurate. This will be discussed later.

In introducing an effective budgeting procedure management has to make a penetrating, critical and uncompromising study of the business to determine its strengths and weaknesses in relation to what it is trying to achieve. First of all it has to test the validity of its objectives in relation to the skills and resources of the business and to the particular competence required for its products and markets.

Management will be looking at the business factually and previously held opinions will be tested against the facts. There will be a better understanding of the key factors and particular skills and resources required to compete successfully. The result of the investigation may be to confirm or to reorientate the objectives. In either event the required standards should emerge for evaluating the strengths and weaknesses.

The examination will normally start with the entrepreneurial activities that constitute the basic elements of a business and which largely condition its success or failure. The results of this investigation will suggest what further examination is necessary.

The entrepreneurial activities may be summed up as products, markets, volume of sales and profit. It is essential for a company to know its sales of each major product in each major market and to compare these against total sales by product and market. Underlying these figures is the need to ascertain the growth potential of each product and the company's share of the market.

1.2   Market

Information on past and present sales performance should be obtained over a period of three to five years wherever practicable and the factors that should normally be taken into account are:

1   The sales by the company of each major product in each
     major market.
2   The total sales of each product in each market, i.e. the
     aggregate sales of all suppliers.
3   The company's share of each market by product lines.
4   The profit from each product line in each market. This
     is especially important where the selling price varies
     with the market.

This analysis will provide a fund of information. In particular
it will show:

1   The most important markets for each product and the
     trend upwards or downwards.
2   The share of the market. This underlines company
     strengths and weaknesses by products and markets and
     indicates trends.

This information will enable a company to determine where
it stands in relation to competition from products and markets. It will also determine the growth pattern, or decline of
each product: in short the products that have a future and the
products that have passed their peak.

The decisive factor in the strength or weakness of a company is the acceptability of the product by the market. Where
the company has a low market rating for its product then it is
usually faced with the major task of redesigning the product
and establishing it in the market. For many products a minimum of two years or more is required to achieve this.

An annual budget, properly undertaken, will expose product-market weaknesses but it cannot generally influence
them in the short term. The fact is that the annual profit
statement can be a short period in the profit cycle of a company. The profit that a company earns in the current year
generally reflects the outcome of major decisions taken two,
three or more years earlier. This is the story behind most of
the successful companies and it leads to a consideration of
the total planning requirements of a business.

1.3   The total planning concept

For most companies long-term planning in addition to annual

budgetary planning is essential to maintain the annual profit at a consistently good or improving level.

The ultimate measure of the success of a business is generally based on the following factors:

1   *Growth in the volume of sales.* A business should ensure that its product lines have a growth potential with an increasing share of the market.

2   *Increasing return on capital investment.* It is important that in the long term the profit earned on the capital employed should show an increasing trend.

3   *Efficient organisation.* The organisation should be maintained at the level of efficiency appropriate to the requirements of the business and with particular regard to technology, product-market demands and the size of the undertaking. Succession should preserve and promote the necessary skills.

These are all long-term considerations.

The period of long-term planning is determined by the lead time generally required to implement a major decision, for example, the time required to launch a new product and establish it in the market. The total planning concept generally embraces the following subdivisions:

Strategic Long-term Planning
Operational Planning
Annual Budgeting

Once a year management should make a penetrating and comprehensive study of the business to see where it stands and what it is capable of doing. On the basis of this information management should decide what changes, if any, should be made to the major objectives of the business and consider the strategy and the means for achieving them with due regard to the lead time for implementation.

Strategic planning with a long-term focus is generally implemented in whole or in part through selected projects, all of which are defined and coordinated in relation to a master plan. Every project will be carefully examined to test its validity and it must, of course, provide an acceptable return on the investment. But it is not the function of strategic planning to measure the profitability of a business; its function is to shape the business and create the foundations for profitable operation.

Operational planning, and to a greater extent budgeting, are responsible for producing the profits but these are very limited indeed unless strategic planning has paved the way by creating the right conditions for profitable operation.

Every company has a need for strategic planning to give timely consideration to such long-term considerations as designing and developing new products or updating existing products, extending markets or breaking into new markets, and enlarging the production plant facilities in anticipation of increasing demands.

Operational planning coordinates all the activities of the business. It implements the strategic decisions, ensuring that they are planned and programmed in accordance with the due dates. If it is the introduction of a new or updated product it will ensure that production commences as scheduled. It will ensure that all methods and procedures necessary for efficient operation have been introduced. It will create standards for monitoring performance. It will ensure that all activities are properly organised and coordinated and that the organisation itself is equal to the demands and responsibilities of the situation.

Operational planning is concerned with qualitative as well as quantitative performance. In this connection it can highlight serious weaknesses which would not be apparent in the budgeting procedure which is geared to quantitative performance. For example, it can highlight an increase in the number of overdue deliveries to customers which may not be reflected in reduced sales.

A budget is not generally concerned with an investigation of sales when these are in line with, or exceed, budget expectations and give no indications of any unusual trends. Yet serious weaknesses may pass undetected. One company maintained its budgeted sales for three years without realising the facts behind the figures. A substantial increase in the sales of spares covered the fact that the company was losing ground in share of the market for its products. This company pinned its faith on annual budgeting without the support of comprehensive operational planning to expose possible weaknesses.

The three main subdivisions of business planning have their respective functions but there are no fixed boundaries as each tends to shade into the other. They are complementary to each other, interdependent and reactionary. Budgeting can expose a weakness in strategic planning and operational planning. Operational planning can expose a weakness in strategic planning and budgeting.

Strategic planning looks at the business largely in terms of projects. It ensures that each project is compatible with the master plan; that it is feasible and will make a worthwhile contribution to the profitability of the undertaking. It operates on the principle that if the constituent parts of the plan are correct for the business the sum of these parts, the total plan, must also be correct. It is not the function of long-term strategic planning to measure and project the profitability of the business for a given period of time.

Operational planning operates on the principle that if all the activities and operations are performed efficiently and economically then the by-product, profit, will emerge. Operational planning will be interested in sectional profitability but it is not a part of its function to measure and project profitability for a future period.

Budgeting is concerned with measuring and projecting profitability for a future period. The budget has not only to take account of competition but it has to consider the short-term effects of all other factors that can influence the trading prospects for the period under review, for example, economic conditions and government restraints. Armed with this information management has to decide the tactics to be adopted in the short term to exploit favourable trading conditions or to counteract an adverse situation.

The phrase 'corporate planning' has been coined in recent years to denote the total planning requirements of a business. While the term is comparatively new the principles have been practised for many years by the most successful companies in America and Europe. But for the majority of companies there was a real need to direct attention to the total requirements of business planning; to show that it was not a management option but an essential discipline and to demonstrate that it was not a piecemeal application but had to be comprehensively and factually applied to the total activities of the business. Corporate planning has publicised the needs but it is an under-developed discipline.

1.4   Corporate planning

Corporate planning is concerned with all factors, certainly all major factors, that can influence the success of a business. It is concerned with policies, objectives, organisation, methods and procedures and the other considerations that stem from them, e.g. standards of performance and control.

1.4.1   Policies

Policies provide a broad framework for the operation of a company. They take the form of statements of management intent on matters of fundamental and long-range significance to the company. Policies are introduced with the object of long-term application. They should not be unchangeable, nor should they be subject to frequent change for then management loses its purpose and sense of direction. Policies give stability and consistency to a company in its decision-making and actions.

The policies that generally have the greatest impact on corporate planning are related to products, markets and marketing. A sound product policy is a means of ensuring that a company has the resources and is competent to produce and market its products or services.

It is not every company that appreciates the value of a carefully thought out product policy clearly defined in a written statement. It is not surprising, therefore, that when companies start to think in terms of sound product policies related to their skills and resources one of the first tasks that often confronts them is a rationalisation of their product lines. These considerations are so important in the management of a company as to justify a product philosophy, as mentioned later.

1.4.2   Objectives

In a company with well articulated policies it follows that objectives must be decided within the framework of those policies which set the guidelines and constraints. Every company should follow the practice of some of the most successful companies and take a close look at the business once a year to decide what should be done to improve its operations. Determining what should be done (objectives), how it should be done (plans), and when it should be done (programmes), together with the financial considerations involved, are essential for every company.

Some of the objectives will be strategic with a long-term focus; others will be tactical and attainable in the short term. Decisions have to be based on a factual approach and the objectives have to be in line with the skills and resources of the company.

Objectives determine the aims and the means for implementing company policies. All objectives, long or short term, serve the common purpose of strengthening the company by enlarging its resources and progressively increasing its sales and profitability. It follows, of course, that not only must the objectives be valid for the company but there must also be the probability of attainment as persons will be held accountable for performance according to their respective responsibilities.

1.4.3   Organisation

The purpose of organisation is to make the best use of human resources both from the viewpoint of the company and of the individuals concerned. It is a question of identifying the jobs to be done and choosing the right persons for the jobs. But it also means helping the person to do the job by ensuring that he has access to the necessary information. Management has to ensure that the various jobs are co-ordinated to produce the end results required.

1.4.4   Methods and procedures

Every company should give careful consideration not only to
the facilities required for a job but to the method of doing
the job. Well thought out methods and procedures expressed
in simple terms and readily available for reference by all concerned makes for efficiency and economy. An organisation
cannot be truly efficient unless it operates in accordance with
established methods and procedures, nor will the right people
be selected for jobs if there is no information to show what
each job involves. Established methods and procedures can
reduce training time and experience shows that they also
permit ordinary people to do extraordinary things (the whole
is greater than the sum of its parts).

1.4.5   Control

It is essential that aims and achievements, plans and performance, can be evaluated and this requires standards of
measurement. Standards have to be qualitative as well as
quantitative. The performance of top management and others
down to supervisory level can be measured quantitatively
through the budget. Qualitative standards are the province
generally of operational planning and control.

Another factor is that control is the key to delegation. Top
management can delegate authority but in doing so it cannot
avoid responsibility. Delegation is therefore dependent upon
the means to control performance.

1.5   Product philosophy

What most companies need is a product philosophy and a
marketing strategy. In this connection it is important at the
outset to define the objectives. For example, one highly
successful international company has stated that its objective
is to sell a particular range of products covering all major
sectors of the market.

What a company cannot afford to happen is a decline in

sales as this will inevitably lead to a reduction of profit. Sales will decline if the market demand for a product is declining, i.e. when a product has passed its peak. Alternatively, sales can decline even when the product itself has a growth potential if the company's share of the market is declining.

For decades iron piping and pipe fittings have been used for heating systems and flowing liquids. In recent years these have been replaced to an extent by plastic piping and this process is expanding. This forces the manufacturer of cast iron piping into the manufacture of plastic piping if he elects to maintain his market and into a large investment in plant since the production techniques and plant requirements are entirely different. He will also have the problem of deciding how to utilise the existing plant which may well represent a fairly large investment.

The above is an example not only of product substitution but of a change in industry. Many companies by the very nature of their products face more or less the same problems and the accelerating pace of industry is reducing the life cycle of a wide range of products. In these circumstances companies have to develop a field of interest compatible with their technology, particular skills, innovatory abilities and resources and have substitute products available as the need arises. This will be fundamental to the success of a business. To delay action until the need is obvious is too late to avoid a sales gap.

There are many companies that make products with a long-term growth potential. Their problem is not to find a new product line but to ensure that their designs are updated to meet market demands. The manufacture of motor cars is a good example. Cars have a long-term growth potential but the models on the market at any time have a short life cycle. Designs have to be regularly updated and can vary from a 'facelift' to a completely new design.

There is a third category where the product is not subject to innovation and can remain unchanged over a long term of years, for example, certain basic chemicals, steel, etc. But few industries can escape the need for innovation. Where it is not the product, it can be the process of manufacture and/or the marketing strategy.

The hard fact is that the market imposes standards and in a

dynamic situation these standards change. Modern conditions do not provide the time for dealing with changes on an *ad hoc* basis; changes have to be anticipated and management requires a product philosophy geared to the particular circumstances of the business to deal with them effectively.

A product philosophy can be effectively developed and coordinated through a product committee representing all the major components of a company and meeting regularly. Its function will be to review and coordinate product design, development, production and marketing. Its objectives will be to ensure that the company recognises the needs and desires of the market far enough ahead to have the right products in the right places at the right time and in the right quantity. Alfred P. Sloan, Junior, one time chief executive of General Motors, said that the ever changing market and ever changing product could break any business organisation if it had not provided procedures for anticipating change.

1.6   Extended budgeting

It is important for a company to see its sales for the next three to five years in terms of products and markets wherever practicable. This is one of the purposes, probably the major purpose, of extended budgeting. Profit enters into it but the figures are expected to be indicative rather than strictly accurate.

Extended budgeting is not a substitute for strategic long-term planning. Strategic planning creates and budgeting monitors. The budget should in fact be a financial interpretation of the strategic plan.

In budgeting three to five years ahead it is customary to prepare a budget for each year. The budget for the first year will be comprehensive as it fixes responsibility and accountability for performance. The budgets for subsequent years will be less detailed as the primary object is to test the validity of the sales figures and to improve, or at least maintain, the current sales level and the related profit. Sales trends by products and markets will be closely studied. Products that show a downward trend will be considered in conjunction with the plans for introducing new or updated products.

1.7   Management by objectives

In recent years much prominence has been given to management by objectives. This has highlighted the benefits to be obtained from formalised, systematic planning applied to the total operations of a company. Its purpose is to identify the key factors for survival and growth; to consider the actions most appropriate to the success of the business and in line with the particular skills, general competence and resources of the company; and to determine the objectives for achieving the best results. It considers the present operations of the company and decides how these should be re-orientated, if necessary. The central theme is to maximise the return on resources.

There is nothing new in management by objectives — progressive companies have been operating this way for many years. But the majority of companies, if aware of it, have certainly never practised it and there is no doubt that its wider application would raise the general standards of management performance.

1.8   Management information services

Anyone doing a job must have access to the information required to do it. The information may be verbal or in writing. In all but the simplest jobs experience shows that written information produces the best results.

Standard operations should be covered by written procedures or guidelines. Repetitive routine operations should generally be covered through step-by-step procedures. In many companies procedures can account for most of the information required to operate the business.

Reports also have an important place in information services. These should be examined periodically to ensure that they are serving a useful purpose. Every examination usually uncovers some reports that are no longer essential. It can also follow that valuable information is not available from the existing reports and this will require attention.

The other information required can best be ascertained from a penetrating and systematic study of the company in its entirety to determine the specific information needed at each particular position in relation to the decisions that have to be made. A typical example is to consider the information required by the marketing director in deciding a sales budget.

Information in companies tends to grow but it is not a cultivated growth. More often than not there is a surfeit of information but a shortage of facts. Management information services tend to get out of hand because the specific requirements have not been systematically established or controlled. Computer applications will make an increasing contribution to management information services.

1.9   The business survey and appraisal

Reference has been made to the need for management to see the business in its true perspective, to know its strengths and weaknesses and to have a clear understanding of the particular competence required to compete successfully in the industry in which it operates. This requires a systematic and comprehensive study of the business. The object at this point is to consider some of the many factors that enter into the appraisal of a business.

1.9.1   Business appraisal

There are many yardsticks that can be used for assessing the performance of a company but probably the most common is the profit and sales record over a period of years. The first point to be noted is whether profits and sales have increased progressively and without interruption in each of those years. The second point is to ascertain whether profits, in relation to the capital investment and to sales, is showing an increasing or diminishing return.

A financial investigation of this kind can be revealing and

indicative but it really highlights effects. To establish causes, an investigation in greater depth is usually required. It is obviously desirable that a company should operate efficiently and establish good profit earnings but at the marginal end of the scale it is also essential that it should survive and preserve its capital investment until improvements can be introduced.

It goes without saying that management should have a comprehensive understanding of its business and of the industry and environment in which it operates but this is by no means common knowledge, even in those companies that are highly profitable.

Management should have an intimate knowledge of product-market performance:

1   The sales of each major product in each major market and share of the market; any important markets for its products which the company has not penetrated and the size of the markets should be known.

2   The growth potential, the frequency of model changes, and the anticipated life cycle of major products.

3   Investment opportunities and priorities in relation to current and prospective products.

4   The type of organisation required to operate the company successfully and how far the existing organisation meets this requirement in the main essentials.

It is the product-market performance that creates the differential between the successful and the average company, between the leaders and the marginal producers. The acceptability of the products in the markets with regard to quality, availability, service and price; the marketing policies and methods, the distribution channels and the marketing organisation — these are the significant factors that determine the product-market performance.

Obviously there are other factors that influence the performance and profitability of a company. The most important factor of all is, or should be, the contribution of top management to the direction and operation of the business. An effective organisation supported and coordinated through planned programmes and well-established practices and procedures is also a vital factor in performance.

Every management must make a clear assessment of the

overall strengths and weaknesses of its company as a prerequisite to profit planning and control. What is required by a company is a far more penetrating and orderly study of the business in its entirety to understand what it is doing and what it is capable of doing and what are its limitations. As a corollary to this, it follows that a company cannot be successful unless it has the skills and resources and the particular competence required for its products and its markets.

1.9.2   The planning framework

What should the objectives of the enterprising company be? —

1   *Growth in the volume of sales.* It is important that the products should have a growth potential and an increasing share of the market.

2   *Increasing return on capital investment.* In the long term the profit earned on the capital invested should show an increasing trend.

3   *Efficient organisation.* The organisation should be maintained at the level of efficiency appropriate to the operations of the business. Succession should preserve and promote the particular skills.

4   *Adequate resources.* The resources (management, men, money and machines) should be equal to the demands of the business.

Is the company organised and equipped to plan for these objectives with a reasonable prospect of attainment? This question can only be answered through a clear understanding and intimate knowledge of the business and this requires a penetrating study of the operations of the business and its performance. It also requires information to show how the business reached its present stage of development.

If a company makes several products it may be that it is in fact operating in more than one business. If the different products are being sold to different customers, or if the production plant and the methods of manufacture are distinctive for each product, or if the competitors in each product line are different, then these are indications that the company is operating in more than one business. A chemical company manufactured four different chemicals and it transpired that each of the products virtually constituted a different business. It is important to identify the different businesses, if any, as a means of analysing and assessing opportunities and the strength of competition.

It follows that other differences will be ascertained from a further analysis; size and extent of the market, the growth rate of the product, share of the market, profitability, and it is almost certain that each product will show a varying pattern.

In establishing the present position of a business two aspects have to be considered; the performance of the business and the environment in which it operates. These may be referred to as the business performance audit and the environment audit.

1.9.3 The business performance audit

The performance of a business is primarily measured by its product sales, market acceptance of the products, or market rating, and profit earnings. There are, of course, other considerations. Sales and profits are results and not causes and if the results are favourable then the principal contributary factors should be known. If the results are unfavourable the causes should be ascertained.

The purpose of the performance audit is to identify strengths and weaknesses. The particular strengths, or competence, required for the successful operation of the business should be identified and the existing organisation checked to see if it measures up to these requirements. If a business is design-orientated then R&D and product design will be particularly important. If the design of the products are relatively standard and with little scope for innovation, then the emphasis may be on production to achieve economic manufacturing costs that will give the company a price advantage; or it may be decided that the company can be best served by marketing orientation through greater marketing penetration, extending the markets, aggressive selling and intensive publicity. At any time the nature of a business is decided by its product lines and markets and these set the limits of opportunity for a company. The skills and resources of a company and the degree of orientation, or particular competence, have to be related to the products and the volume of sales. The need is, therefore, for a balanced organisation that is product/market orientated.

If a company aims at extending its product lines to increase its area of opportunity then it must make a fresh appraisal of skills, particular competence, and resources because these at all times must measure up to the particular demands of the products.

The performance audit has to make a penetrating and impartial examination of, the total operations of a company. The audit will dictate the aspects of the business that require particular study but it will generally have to provide answers to these typical questions:

1.   What is the probable life cycle of the existing products?

    (a)   What products have a growth potential? What is the anticipated growth rate of each product (expressed as an annual percentage increase)?

    (b)   What products have passed their peak? What is the anticipated rate of decline (expressed as annual percentage)?

2   What are the specific strengths and weaknesses of the major product lines? These should be identified and analysed in terms of each major market. The object is to evaluate sales volume and share of market and to identify competative strengths and weaknesses in products and markets.

3   How are markets changing? Are buying habits changing, are the market demands changing, are distribution channels changing? These are just a few of the many factors that can change markets and a company must be aware of them.

4   Is competition changing? Is the industry subject to changes through acquisition and mergers with new and powerful companies entering the market? What are the other factors that are changing the competative outlook?

5   Has the company a product philosophy? Is design and product development ahead or behind competition?

6   How effective is present management? Is it experienced and skilled in the particular business and industry in which the company operates?

7   How effective is the present organisation as a coordinated work-force? Is it weak in any particular sector?

8   Does the organisation operate through well established disciplines imposed by planned objectives with account-ability for performance? Is the organisation supported by properly planned procedures and practices? Have standards of performance been established for all major and key operations? Is the responsibility of individuals clearly defined?

9   Is management sophisticated in planning procedures? Does it accept the importance of planning and the need to delegate responsibility for implementing the various sections of the plan?

10   Is it appreciated that top management without efficient and cooperative departmental management spells weak overall management? Are departmental managers care-fully selected, adequately trained and given the status commensurate with the job?

11   How good is worker morale?

These are only a typical sample of the questions that have to be answered with a view to ascertaining the strengths and weaknesses of the company.

One of the statements that will emerge from the examin-ation will be a record of performance over the past three to five years. This will normally show the sales of each major product in each major market for each year. It will show wherever practical the total demand for each product in each market and from this the company's share of each market will be calculated. The figures for each market will be summarised to give the total view. Another useful statement is to show the cost of each product in the years under review. This is usually developed to show the selling price (average) of each product in each year, also the manufacturing cost (materials cost *plus* production cost) and the difference between the two figures shows the factory contribution to profit. This indicates the profitability of each product.

Statements of this kind are particularly useful; it shows

the comparative sales volume of each product and its contribution to profit; it shows the growth pattern, if any, for each product and its consistency or otherwise; it pinpoints the marginal products.

1.9.4   The environment audit

The environment audit can be approached from several viewpoints. It can be approached from the competative environment and the conditions, or trading environment. The competitive angle is obvious; the conditions environment relates to economic, social, political and legislative conditions, all of which have an influence on the trading environment.

Competition must be assessed for each major product in each major market. Taking each product in turn the information required for each market will generally relate to:

1   *The number of competitors and their share of the market.* There may, for example, be 14 competitors but 80 per cent of the market may be shared by three competitors. The three competitors will be placed in market rating order as measured by their respective sales volumes.

2   *Technology.* If the product is a technological one then the technological strength of the major competitors must be assessed. Referring to the three major producers above as an example it would be necessary to rate them technologically and this rating may not coincide with the market rating.

3   *Resources.* The resources of each major competitor have to be assessed because the company with the greatest resources may hold the key to leadership in the market if it is not already established as the leader. Referring again to the three major producers these would have to be rated according to the assessment of resources. It could be that the rating of the three companies for sales volume, technological strength and resources vary. This could be an indication that the present market leader is being challenged for leadership.

The conditions environment will from time to time create

a favourable or unfavourable trading climate. These conditions will affect all competitors but the leaders will probably be better placed to benefit from a favourable climate and to minimize the effects of an unfavourable climate.

1.9.5   The management programme

The results of these studies will indicate or imply a course of action for top management. The business performance audit will show the strengths and expose the weaknesses inherent in the current operations of the company and will project the need for management action. The environment audit will highlight the opportunities and the threats that confront the company, again demonstrating the need for management action.

Top management will, or should be, sufficiently skilled to interpret the results of these studies and to decide the actions to be taken to strengthen the company internally and externally. But there has to be a systematic approach to applying corrective measures. All the points for action should be listed and it can be expected that these will be grouped under one of two categories, or more: *(a)* points decided and *(b)* points for consideration. Matters affecting the internal operations of the company, for example, the re-organisation and strengthening of the marketing division will appear under 'points decided'. Matters affecting the company externally generally require further consideration and will be listed under 'points for consideration'. The important factor emerging from all this is that top management is in the process of creating the framework of a management programme. The points decided upon for action will be listed in the priority in which they should be undertaken. A target date for implementation will be decided for each and the responsibility for implementation will normally be assigned to the head of the division affected by it. Progress reports will require to be submitted at stated intervals.

The points that require further consideration will be listed according to the priority to be given to each and these will remain the responsibility of top management until decisions are made and action can be delegated.

1.9.6 The planning philosophy

Projecting a plan that will improve the prospects and the performance of a company and increase the profits at a satisfactory rate is one of the primary objectives of planning and it is probably the most important function and responsibility of top management.

The plan should span a minimum period of three years but for most companies a five-year plan will probably be more representative.

Logically the starting point of the planning procedure is to project the prospects of the present business operating on the same basis through existing products and markets. This forecast will have to take into account the growth rate of each product and share of the market.

Top management will decide if the results forecasted provide a reasonable sales and profit growth. If the forecasts are generally acceptable a progressive management will consider what can be done to consolidate those prospects and possibly improve them. Considerations for improving performance will generally take account of such factors as improving the products, more intensive selling, finding new markets for the products and generally improving competitive position and share of the market. Concentrating on selling more of the most profitable products is another consideration that generally arises but this can be a difficult and unrewarding task.

If the growth prospects through the existing products are unsatisfactory then management will have to consider what new products can be developed or acquired to sell in present markets. Management will have to consider the skills, particular competence and resources of the company and its market standing relative to competition to ensure that it can justify adding these new products to its existing lines.

In addition, or as an alternative, management may well consider new products for sale in new markets. Although this can be more difficult than selling new products in present markets it can be warranted if the company is particularly competent in R&D technology in a particular field or if it is outstandingly efficient in production or marketing.

Decisions affecting the introduction of new products can-

Strategic Planning to create the conditions for profitability and growth	Operational Planning and Control	Annual Budget Plan
Plans for allocating resources to missions	To plan, coordinate and control the operations of the business	To realise the profit potential created by strategic planning and operational planning with due regard to the current prospects and trading conditions
Markets and marketing plans and programmes	To implement the strategic planning projects and the annual budget plan	
Product development programme		

Production development plans and programmes for improving and expanding production facilities	To direct and control every function and activity including:
	  Marketing
	  R&D
	  Production
	  Finance
	  Administration	

Plan of the organisation	To plan manpower requirements and training programmes	
Plans for personnel development	To determine methods, practices and procedures	

Long-term Budgeting to Monitor Strategic Planning

	Year	1	2	3	4	5
Sales						
Cost of Sales						
Gross Profit						
Special Expenditure						
Capital Expenditure						

Note: Sales are obtained from an analysis of sales by products and markets which takes into account the dates of introducing new products and eliminating existing products. It also takes account of market developments

Figure 1.1   Corporate planning

not be delayed unduly as by admission, the performance of the company will be unsatisfactory until new products are introduced. Pending decisions these matters will appear on the management programme.

When all matters have been resolved top management will define the objectives of the company for the next five years. This will become the basis of the management programme for the next five years. Management will assign the tasks associated with the implementation of this programme to the individuals and departments in accordance with their respective functions and accountability for performance will be inherent in every assignment. Management will assign tasks and delegate authority but final responsibility for implementation rests exclusively with top management.

Up to this point only strategic planning has been considered — the planning of those factors which have a major impact and a long term influence on the operations of a company and its performance — and this is generally referred to as corporate planning. Corporate planning or creating the 'master plan', coordinates all other planning within the company.

1.10   Summary

Budgeting is the final process in a comprehensive planning network. An annual budget is the tip of the iceberg that has to be supported by strategic planning in depth in the preceding years and by operational planning in the current year to make it successful as measured by sales and profit.

Shareholders, investors, creditors and the public at large have to judge the performance of a company through its annual published accounts. But a year can be a short period in the profit cycle of most companies. The profit earned in the current year will in most cases be influenced by decisions made and action taken two, three or more years earlier. Equally failure to make decisions currently to protect the future of the company may only be reflected in the annual accounts in three or four years time.

Comprehensive business planning, commonly termed corporate planning, embraces strategic planning with a long-term focus, operational planning and control which does not operate within any determined time limit but is conditioned by the particular requirements of a company, annual budget and long-term budgeting.

All planning has to be coordinated to meet the requirements of the master plan and in most cases, if not in every case, this is the province of operational planning and control which has to operate in accordance with priorities and programmed dates.

Strategic planning creates the conditions for profitable operation and growth. Long-term budgeting monitors strategic planning to ensure that it meets the financial requirements of management in terms of sales, profitability and growth. The annual budget is charged with the task of realising the profit potential created by strategic planning. Operational planning and control embraces every aspect and every activity in the operation of the business. It has to implement the strategic plans and the annual budget plan, and it has to direct and control every operation of the business.

Figure 1.1 gives an outline of corporate planning. In this outline a reference is made to the application of resources to missions. A company may be operating in several fields each constituting a separate business. A chemical company may, for example, operate in three distinct fields; agricultural, industrial and consumer. Here three distinct missions are identified and a company has to decide how to allocate its resources to each to obtain the greatest advantage.

2 Major Considerations in Budgeting

One of the primary objects of an annual budget is to measure the profit expectations for the next financial year with due regard to all the circumstances, favourable and unfavourable, that can influence the trading prospects. Management has to find the answers to the following questions: How should the business operate during the next financial year? What can we hope to achieve? What tactics should we adopt to achieve it? If the profit projected by the budget is unsatisfactory, and particularly if it is likely to fall short of the profit for the current year, management then has to have second thoughts.

Profits do not emerge of their own accord — they have to be influenced by management. The quality of management is often judged by the size of the profit figures at the end of the financial year. For its own protection and in the interests of the business, management must plan to make profit and the accepted basis for this is the annual budget, properly supported by long-term strategic planning and operational planning.

Reference has been made to long-term budgets. First of all it has to be appreciated that long-term budgets are not a substitute for long-term strategic planning as they serve entirely different purposes. A company should endeavour to see its volume of sales in terms of products and markets for the next three to five years. It is the function of strategic planning to ensure the products and the markets and it is the function of long-term budgeting to evaluate the potential sales and to give an indication of profit levels. Long-term budgeting supplements and is a check on strategic planning far enough ahead for timely and appropriate action to be taken if necessary.

It has been seen that strategic planning in conjunction with operational planning should build profit potential into a business — a satisfactory sales volume through a suitable range of products, established markets with an adequate share of the markets; the necessary production facilities and an effective and economical organisation. But creating the conditions for profitable operation is one thing, realising the profit is another and this is the unique function of budgeting on an annual basis.

Identifying and measuring the effects of short-term fluctuations that can influence the immediate trading prospects are the essence of effective budgeting. Long-term trends can often be forecast with greater accuracy than short-term trends but in annual budgeting it is the short-term trends that matter. An industry may state with a reasonable degree of accuracy that there will be a 20 per cent growth in the next five years. It would hardly be expected, however, that the growth rate would be constant each year. Annual budgeting must aim at establishing and evaluating the likely effects of inconsistencies in the period under review.

2.1   A budgeting rationale

Budgeting is a function of top management and unless this is recognised a company will be denied the full benefits of a budgeting procedure. It has to be top-management inspired and motivated. A budget imposes operational standards with accountability for performances and it must be set with these objectives in view.

Budgeting is a coordinated process that affects every aspect of the business and every section of the organisation. It is important to ensure that the budgeting scheme is comprehensive and effective and that the members of the organisation know their responsibilities under the scheme; what has to be done, how it should be done, and how performance will be measured

These requirements are fulfilled through comprehensive written procedures. The particular advantages of a budget manual in this connection will be considered later.

Some of the questions that have to be considered in drafting procedures are:

1   What budgets are included in the scheme? Who is responsible for preparing them and for coordinating them? What is the due date for the completion of each budget?
2   What decisions have to be made in the preparation of each budget?
3   What information will be required to guide these decisions?
4   What are the sources of this information? How will it be collated, analysed and interpreted to establish the facts?

The procedures will be based on a factual approach to decision making and in this connection it has to be appreciated that decisions based on incomplete information can be as misleading as those based on wrong information.

The procedures will give guidance on the preparation of each budget together with a pro-forma. The procedure for considering and approving budgets will be described. A section of the procedures will deal with controls; the methods of comparing actual performance against budget will be described and a pro-forma of each control statement given. The control statements will measure performance in relation to responsibilities.

A few years ago a group of European experts visited many American firms selected for their good managerial practices, and this was their comment:

'Forecasts and estimates are not new to the business world . . . . What is original in America is the precision of the methods used, the budgets being drawn up on the basis of a meticulous and systematic analysis of the component industrial and commercial operations. Few European companies draw up budgets in this meticulous way or use them as an instrument of management control.'

The aim of every company should be to prepare its budgets meticulously, systematically and factually and as an instrument of management control. Furthermore it should aim at a high level of achievement through properly planned and well articulated procedures.

2.2 A budget manual

A manual contains all the procedures that are associated with the budget scheme and all the essential information required for the operation of the scheme.

The manual is usually subdivided into sections to show the procedures particular to each major division of the business. The appropriate section of the manual is issued to each division. There is certain information, however, that is common to the business as a whole and this is incorporated in the manual of every division.

The general information contained in every manual will deal with such matters as:

1   The objectives of budgeting: their purpose, their advantages and the concepts and principles to be observed.
2   Classification of the budgets incorporated in the total scheme.
3   An organisation chart of top level management including heads of divisions with an outline of their responsibilities in the budget scheme.
4   Budget committee: the composition of the committee, its purpose and an outline of the duties it has to perform.
5   The inter-relationship of budgets: a brief description of the dependence of one budget on another, for example, the dependence of the production budget on the sales budget.
6   Management information services: a brief description of the services available and the sections of the organisations responsible for providing them.
7   Timetable for the completion of budgets. Some budgets cannot be started until others are completed. This applies to the production budget which is dependent upon the sales budget.
8   Due dates for the completion of budgets are essential.

The information particular to each division generally incorporates the following:

9   An organisation chart of the division with a brief description of the duties and responsibilities.
10   The information required to prepare the budget.
11   The procedure for preparing the budget.
12   Guidelines on the particular points to be watched and the checks to be applied.
13   A pro-forma of the budget statement.
14   The controls to be exercised to compare actual performance against budget, together with pro-formas of the control statements.

2.3   The master budget and its sub-divisions

The master budget is the profit and loss statement for the next financial year, or other period covered by the budget. This is frequently accompanied by a balance sheet.

It is customary for each major division to prepare its own budget. These divisions are not synonymous in every company but they usually comprise the marketing division, the technical division, which includes product design, development and research, the production division, the financial division and the general administration division.

The budgets generally prepared are listed below:

2.3.1   The marketing division

It is customary for this division to prepare two budgets: a sales budget and an operating costs budget. The sales budget shows, wherever practicable, the sales of each product in each market in terms of physical units and value. The operating costs budget shows the costs of operating the marketing division for the period suitably classified under various expense headings for control purposes.

2.3.2   The technical division

It is customary in this division to have a programme of the

projects that have to be undertaken in the budget period. The programme shows the priority of each project and frequently indicates as a general guide an estimate of the man-hours involved in each project. This information largely decides the manpower requirements and, therefore, the payroll of the division. Some projects may involve or give rise to special purchases. These are usually detailed against each project and a summary will give the total expenditure to be incurred in the period under review.

The policy of a company with regard to the treatment of the total costs of operating the technical division will decide the contents and make-up of the budget. Some companies write off the total expenditure of operating the technical division in the year it is incurred. The annual budget will show the total operating cost in terms of payroll, special purchases, and other expenses appropriate to the operation of the division suitably classified under clearly defined headings for control.

Some companies cost each project on the basis of time and materials and may compare the actual cost against a pre-determined or estimated cost. In such circumstances a company may only show the general operating costs in the annual nudget of the division, namely the costs that are not charged to projects. The project costs may be capitalised and written-off to cost of sales over an extended period. Practice can vary in the capitalisation and amortisation of project costs.

2.3.3   The production division

This division prepares a production budget from the details shown on the sales budget. The first stage is to compare the sales volume plus the inventory requirements with the total production capacity of the plant. The budgeted production volume and production capacity have to be reconciled before the production budget can be completed.

The production budget will show:

Total output in terms of products.

The production materials cost of obtaining the output.

The operating costs of the division.

Several subsidiary budgets are prepared as a step to preparing the production budget. The operating costs, for example, usually involve:

A manpower budget.

A payroll budget, developed from the manpower budget.

An expenses budget.

The production budget will be considered in detail in a later chapter where reference will also be made to the procedure to be adopted by companies that do not manufacture standard products.

2.3.4   The financial division

This division generally performs a dual function: first, it prepares a budget of the operating costs of its division; secondly, it coordinates the information provided by the other divisional budgets to prepare a profit and loss statement, balance sheet, capital expenditure budget and cash flow statement.

2.3.5   The general administration division

In many companies the budget of the operating costs of this division are incorporated with the operating costs of the financial division or vice versa. Size of the divisions may warrant separate budgets. The successful operation of a budget plan requires certain conditions:

1   Top management direction and involvement.
2   An effective organisation with authorities and responsibilities clearly defined.
3   A factual approach to budgeting based on accurate and precise information and pertinent data.
4   A definite plan for the preparation and administration of the budget.
5   Carefully planned and well articulated procedures.
6   A definition of the standards that will be used to measure actual performance against budget in terms of the accountability of individuals.
7   An efficient accounting system for providing the account-

ing information required to operate the budgeting scheme both in preparing and implementing the budgets and in measuring performance. Other controls as required.

8   A statement of the changes that have to be made in current operations to achieve the budgeted objectives. This can be very important as conditions are never static. Every year will bring changes and the need for a company to adapt itself to change.

2.4   Budget philosophy

Notwithstanding all that has been said, a company will not be wholly successful in its application of budgeting unless it has the right attitude, or philosophy. The philosophy should be 'the utmost care and consideration in deciding and approving budgets and maximum involvement in implementing them'.

Some years ago Harlow Curtice, then President of General Motors, testified before a Senate sub-committee investigating the dealer practices of the automobile industry. Commenting upon the reasons for the success of General Motors he made certain references to corporate planning that would equally apply to budgeting:

'Now we come to the second fundamental reason for the success of General Motors — our approach to problems. It is really an attitude of mind. It might be defined as bringing the research point of view to bear on all phases of the business. This involves, first, assembling all the facts, second, analysis of where the facts appear to point, and third, courage to follow the trail indicated even if it leads into unfamiliar and unexplored territory.'

2.5   Budget administration

The size of a company can influence the budget organisation. The normal procedure is to form a committee that is headed preferably by the chief executive and which includes an executive from each division together with a budget coordinator.

The budget coordinator may be an assistant to the chief executive or a senior member of the financial division or other responsible officer. His duties will include:

1   Co-operating with the head of each division to ensure the supply of information required by him to prepare the divisional budget.
2   Equally to ensure that the division has the information it requires to prepare the budget.
3   Ensuring that the completed budgets are available by the due date and prepared in the standard form as shown by the pro-formas. Obtain from each divisional executive any supplementary information that will aid or guide the committee.
4   Presenting the various budgets to the committee in accordance with the nominated dates.
5   Following up any recommendations or revisions made by the committee and ensuring their implementation by the due dates for presentation.

This is an outline of the procedure involved in presenting budgets for approval. Once the budgets are approved the committee may cease to function until the following year. However, in some companies the committee functions throughout the year through regular meetings. The object here is to first approve the budgets and then to receive periodic reports on performance with a view to making appropriate comments and recommendations.

An important point is that administration can take many forms and it must be organised to suit the particular needs and conditions of each company.

2.6   Budget revisions

Many companies are now adopting the principle that once an annual budget has been approved it will not be changed. There is much to commend this practice. It is comparatively simple to establish the deviations from budget and the reasons for them. Frequent budget revisions can result in loss of purpose and sense of direction with no constant standards for measuring performance.

Long-term budgets for ensuring the future of the business are revised and updated annually.

Experience shows that an annual budget will seldom, if ever, be implemented in its original form. The purpose of efficient budgeting is to substantially achieve the aims of the budget while recognising that the means of achieving them are certain to differ. There are few budgets that could not justify revision if these were viewed from a theoretical instead of a practical viewpoint.

One has only to look at any sales budget and the many variables it contains to verify this statement. Most companies sell several products in several markets and the sales budget has to project a sales mix for each market. A sales budget that is meticulously, systematically and factually prepared will project a sales mix and total sales for each market and management will accept these projections in approving the budget. But an experienced management knows that there will be deviations from the approved budget. It also knows in an efficient budgeting environment that there will be less deviations from the approved budget than from any other projection that could be made.

The one factor above all others that can affect budget expectations is a trading recession and reduced sales. In these conditions management has to avoid making short term expediency decisions that can have adverse long term repercussions on the operations of the company. Maintaining an efficient organisation intact is one of the primary objectives of management. It generally follows, unless the recession is unusually severe and protracted, that the marketing and product design divisions will remain intact and the same will apply normally to the financial and general administration divisions. It is in the production division that management is generally confronted with major problems.

In a declining sales order position the level of the order book has to be constantly reviewed. If it is essential to have unexecuted orders equivalent to, say, one month's output to provide the necessary lead time for production then a problem arises when orders fall below this level. It is important, of course, to make sure the decline is common to the industry and not particular to the company as this can involve long-term implications.

A company manufacturing standard products will probably augment its orders by producing for stock over a period. It may also reduce or eliminate overtime working. If the recession is severe or protracted other measures may be necessary.

The important point is that management decisions will be reflected in the production programmes and these can be the basis of short-term production budgets. Through these budgets the position is always under control as mentioned later.

An important factor in budgeting is to prepare a profit and loss statement monthly (or other short-term period) to show the profit earned against budgeted profit for the month and for the year to date. This is a straightforward comparison of management plans and actual achievement. Budget revisions in the course of the year can complicate this comparison.

The budgeting perspective indicates that the sales budget, the technical budget and the financial and administration budgets are not usually revised. Indeed there appears to be no valid purpose served in revising them. The production budget is not so straightforward. Here again the annual budget need not be revised if it is supplemented by a short term production budget which evaluates changes and measures performance. This theme will be developed in subsequent chapters.

In modern business circumstances and conditions can vary considerably and what suits one company may not suit another. In issues such as revision of budgets, management requirements must be the deciding factor.

2.7   The complications of expense behaviour

Identifying expense behaviour is usually associated with production costs as it is in this area that expenditure is greatest and the need for control most essential. For this reason volume of output is usually taken as the basis for defining expense behaviour.

Expenses are normally classified under three headings:

1   Variable expenses.
2   Partly variable expenses.
3   Fixed expenses.

A variable expense is one that changes in almost direct proportion to production output. If output doubled the expense would probably double. This type of expense bears a constant relation to output, for example, materials.

Partly variable expenses vary with output but only at intervals and it generally requires a fairly large fluctuation in output to affect them, for example salaries.

Fixed expenses are not affected by changes in output. Examples are rent, depreciation of buildings and building repairs, etc.

The effect of expense behaviour is that the total expenditure does not increase in proportion to an increase in output and, perhaps more important, does not decrease in proportion to a reduction in output. The annual budget gives no guidance in the control of expenditure where the level of output differs from the budgeted level. The device for the control of expenditure at varying levels of output is the flexible budget which is referred to later.

It has to be appreciated that the control of expenditure cannot be applied with mathematical precision even if the mathematics are correct.

Company policy and management judgement may interfere with or arrest expenditure control in the stricter sense during a recession. In a human situation management will be cautionary in its approach in so far as conditions will permit.

2.8   Static and flexible budgets

A flexible budget is often introduced to operate in conjunction with the annual budget. Unlike the annual budget, which being static shows the expenditure related to a fixed volume of output, the flexible budget shows the expenditure appropriate to various levels of output. If the volume changes the expenditure appropriate to it can be established from the flexible budget and compared with actual expenditure as a means of control. The control of expenditure through a flexible budget is generally confined to production operating costs.

A flexible budget is not a substitute for an annual budget. It requires an annual budget to guide management in its plans to realise a profit that will match its opportunities. The assessment of opportunities, translated into sales income and profit, is the function of an annual budget.

A flexible budget is in effect an expense control budget and, therefore, performs a limited function. In recent years there has been a growing tendency to introduce a short-term fixed budget applied to a programmed production output. As an alternative to flexible budgeting the short-term budget has the advantage that it controls production performances as well as expenditure. Flexible budgeting is operating effectively in a number of companies and Fig. 2.1 shows the principle with a few expenses taken as an example.

The short-term fixed budget which is used in the planning and control of production output and operating costs is based on a definite volume of output as defined by the actual production programme for the period. In the short-term budget

FLEXIBLE BUDGET - PRODUCTION COSTS

Department _____

Period _____   Cost centre _____

Expenses	Fixed/ Variable	Capacity, %			
		70	80	90	100
		£	£	£	£
Direct labour	V	1400	1600	1800	2000
Indirect labour	V	800	840	880	920
Supervision	F	220	220	220	220
Supplies	V	240	250	260	270
Loose tools	V	200	215	230	245
Power and light	V	180	195	210	225
Repairs and maintenance	V	220	220	240	240
Depreciation of plant	F	450	450	450	450
Establishment charges	F	120	120	120	120
TOTAL		3830	4110	4410	4690

Figure 2.1   Flexible budger

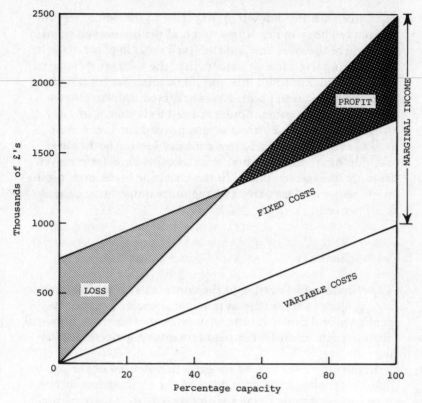

*Figure 2.2   Product life cycle sales and profit during the lifetime
of a product*

the emphasis is on output and since operating costs are
relatively fixed any failure to obtain it represents a loss.

2.9   Profit/volume charts

Charts are sometimes used in budgeting for the graphic presentation of profit-volume relationships. These are also
referred to as break-even charts and a typical example is
given in Fig. 2.2. It is customary to show capacity on the
horizontal scale and money on the vertical scale. Costs are
subdivided into fixed and variable costs and plotted in ac-

cordance with the amount appropriate to the percentage of capacity. The sales line is inserted and the break-even point falls where the sales line and the fixed costs line intersect. It has to be appreciated, of course, that the sales are calculated on a particular product mix and if the mix changes it will alter the break-even point. Also that fixed and variable expenses are an assessment only and not a statement of fact.

A company is in a strong position when the break-even occurs at a comparatively low capacity level. Another indication of strength is where normal capacity is far removed from the break-even point. In the chart the break-even occurs at 40 per cent of capacity and the normal operating capacity is 80 per cent.

2.10   Summary

The purpose of budgeting in the context of an annual budget is to project as accurately as possible the sales income, expenditure and profit for the ensuing year. This is the principal objective and all the other requirements of budgeting stem from it.

Budgeting should assess the growth potential of the product lines and project total sales demand for each market. It must then project company sales with due regard to share of the markets after taking account of competition and technological developments. Trading prospects have to be taken into account; how will economic and social conditions and trends, not ignoring the action of governments, influence the potential sales in the period under review?

Budgeting must be meticulous, systematic and factual and it has to be recognised as an instrument of management for directing and controlling the operations of the business. Management is responsible for the budget and for the results achieved against it. Budgeting embraces every aspect of the business and every section of the organisation and the preparation of the appropriate budgets has to be delegated to divisional levels together with responsibility and accountability for performance. Budgets must be set with these objectives in view. Control is exercised through periodical financial statements and reports.

Complications in the control of the expenditure of the production division can arise where actual output differs from the budgeted output. In these circumstances actual expenditure cannot be compared on a pro-rata basis with budgeted expenditure because of the incidence of fixed and partly variable expenses. The control of expenditure at varying levels of output can be effected through a flexible budget or a short-term production budget. Wherever practicable the short-term production budget is to be preferred as it gives control over production performance as well as expenditure.

Some companies usually those sophisticated in the art of budgeting will not revise an annual budget once it is approved and there can be much to commend this. They reason that the budgeting procedure with the comparisons it provides would not be improved by revising the budget. They contend that, by allowing the budget to run its course, more useful and meaningful comparisons and information can be obtained.

3 The Marketing Function

In recent years the term marketing has taken the place of what used to be known as the sales operation. This is not simply a change of title. It is a reflection of the increasing sophistication that has been forced on companies to meet the ever changing conditions and complexities of business operations. It not only affects marketing but extends to the total operations of a business.

Increased objectivity and closer coordination of the associated activities are only two of the many changes that have been brought about through changing events. In marketing this has resulted in the recognition and coordination of every activity that can influence sales.

Perhaps the one factor that has made the greatest impact on marketing is that the manufacturer can no longer determine what the product should be without a close study of the needs and demands of the user. Marketing in the new concept has to influence a company in what it should make to meet market demands.

The motor car industry and particularly the Ford model 'T' provides a historical example of what can happen to a company if it persists in usurping the function of the user. Henry Ford had the idea of mass producing a car at a price low enough to bring it within the reach of the masses. For many years the car dominated the market. In the twenty years that the car was retained on the market the American economy developed enormously as did the spending power of the masses and the model 'T' was outdated. Henry Ford was slow to recognise the change in outlook and lost his established lead in the market.

Misjudging the needs of the customer is not a thing of the past but a recurring feature of business operation. Most companies are fully aware of the need to study the wants of the customer in designing their products but while this is an obvious safeguard it carries no guarantee.

A customer is not articulate in his wants or desires. His preferences are expressed in his selection from the products that are available to him. His wants can only be ascertained through a study of what he buys. Again a customer does not always recognise real value in a product, he may sacrifice quality or performance for appearance.

Manufacturers have to identify the trends and try to anticipate the desires of the customer. How to build greater customer appeal into the product at an acceptable price is the problem and there are few companies (including some of the largest and most influential) that have not misjudged on occasions. Some companies recognise this requirement of anticipating customer needs as a discipline in its own right and have developed a product philosophy as mentioned later.

Marketing is the 'eyes and ears' of a business and it is responsible for keeping the company in close contact with its environment and informed on events that can influence its operations.

3.1 The marketing function: what it is

To say that the purpose of a company is to create a customer is altogether too naive. The purpose of a business is to create a source of income and to go on increasing it. This requires a critical appraisal of the particular skills and competence required in relation to the product or service that is being provided or contemplated. An assessment has to be made of the volume of sales necessary to make the business profitable, the ease or difficulty of entering the market, and the possibility of attaining the required level of sales. There is also the question of providing the financial resources necessary to support the level of activity.

Only when a company has a product or service to sell that is acceptable to the market is it in a position to identify its potential customers.

This searching analysis is not only necessary at the inception of a company but should be repeated regularly, certainly at least once a year, to ensure that policies, objectives and products or services are marketing-orientated. This is one of the major contributions of marketing to the progress of a business. A company has to continue to justify a place in the market through its products or services and must be capable of selling these at prices and in sufficient volume to make an economic profit, i.e. a profit that will provide a reasonable return on the capital investment and permit the company to maintain at least its competitive position.

The more detailed activities in the marketing function are considered below.

3.2   The sales organisation

The type of product, the sales outlets and the volume of sales can influence the nature and the size of the sales organisation. Many companies have to decide on a reasonable compromise between direct sales representation, selling through agents and advertising.

In selling consumer products through retailers advertising may have the greatest influence. In any case the manufacturer likes to establish some relationship with the user and advertising coupled with a brand name can serve this purpose. In selling products to industrial users direct, sales representation may be the best answer. One advantage of employing fully trained sales representatives is that valuable information can be obtained from the field regarding products, competitors' activities and the market standing of the company. This can be an important factor of marketing intelligence. The number of sales representatives to be employed is usually decided in the first place by the number of customers and the frequency of call. Customers are often graded into categories according to the annual value of their purchases and the frequency of call decided for each category. This may vary from monthly calls in the top category down to half-yearly or no calls at all in the lowest category. The other factor is the number of calls per day that a representative is expected to make on average. This provides a reasonable basis for determining the number to be employed but it does not usually end there. Other factors enter into it which may have the effect of increasing or decreasing this number. The time a representatives is expected to spend in obtaining new customers can, for example, increase the number of representatives.

The size of the sales force can influence the manner in which it operates. In one medium-sized company employing more than 100 representatives there were area representatives with an area sales manager in charge of each area. The product can influence the type or calibre of representatives to be employed. There will be a distinction in the low priced product and the very expensive product and in technical products that require technical representation.

Records have to be maintained for each representative and each sales area. If the sales representative is given a sales quota for his territory then the orders obtained or actual sales (whichever is the basis) will be compared with his quota monthly and for the year to date. In some cases the sales quota is detailed by product lines and the sales achieved are shown on the same basis. Other information may be shown on the monthly statement, for example, average number of calls per day and cost per call.

It is usual to incorporate the statement for each representative into a summarised statement for the sales area and the area sales manager comments on area performance in a monthly report to the sales manager. The area statements are summarised in a monthly statement of total sales. The sales manager submits a monthly report to the marketing director who in turns presents a monthly report to the board.

The sales operation should never be planned or organised in isolation. It should operate within the framework and fulfil the objectives of the marketing policies and strategic aims.

3.3 Distribution channels

Deciding the distribution channels that are most appropriate
to a product line can be a major decision with important con-
sequences. Distribution can take many forms. Certain
consumer goods may be customarily sold through wholesalers unless the accounts are large enough to sell direct to
retailers as with supermarkets. Other goods may be sold direct
to retailers or manufacturers may operate through their own
retail shops. Products may be sold through established distributors. Some products are sold direct to the users particularly to industrial users. A cosmetics manufacturer sells the
products direct to housewives in door-to-door calls by sales-
women. Three different companies making small tools, drills,
taps and the like, differ in their dsitribution policies; one sells
to users only, another to stockists only and the third to
stockists generally but also to users where the size of the
account justifies this direct approach.

Companies can make mistakes in their channels of distribution and these can be costly. It is an area that requires
careful study before any major commitments are undertaken.

3.4 Physical distribution

The costs of physical distribution are now attracting more
attention as they can represent a substantial proportion of
the total cost. In some industries the cost of distribution is
greater than the cost of production. For many years production costs have been closely controlled but until recently
distribution costs have been largely taken for granted.

The closer study of distribution costs has led companies to
a consideration of the various alternatives and these can
involve some complex problems. Distribution for many
companies can mean operating a large number of transport
vehicles and using depots. The problem is to strike the right
balance between the number of vehicles and the number of
depots and their location to obtain the optimum service at
the optimum costs.

This is a wide and complex study.

3.5   Advertising

In many industries the increase in sales to be derived from advertising can be questionable. Some companies serving the consumer product market attach particular importance to advertising in their marketing strategy and spend large sums annually. In these cases top management gives close attention and consideration to the advertising and it is strongly supported by product innovation. There is no doubt that in these particular companies this strategy does pay.

The majority of companies adopt an advertising programme that is generally dictated by what they might lose to competition if they did not advertise rather than by what they might gain from it.

There is an aura of doubt concerning advertising — how to assess the benefits, if any, arising from it. There are, of course, legitimate reasons for advertising. A new company has to make its existence and its products known to potential customers. Companies that sell through intermediaries resort to advertising to make their names and their beanded goods known to users. Advertising is frequently adopted to launch new products and to bolster the sales of products that are declining pending new products being introduced. Where there are no obvious benefits obtained from advertising, companies for the most part are prepared to allocate an annual sum for it generally based on a fixed percentage of sales.

3.6   Marketing research

The foremost need of management to operate a business successfully is to be well-informed. Management systems must of necessity be basically concerned with acquiring and interpreting better data.

The most direct and probably the principal sources available to most companies for obtaining information are through the field contacts of the sales representatives and from market research.

Market research has established itself as a valuable tool for providing essential information as an aid to management decisions. But it usually deals with specific projects, for example, a survey of a new market that a company may be considering. While it satisfies the specific needs of a business in its usual application it does not always provide the general information required by management to guide the operations of the business.

The market research process has to be extended to provide marketing intelligence or be supplemented by another arrangement. Marketing intelligence does not focus on particular projects or problems but establishes sources of regular information relevant to a company's operations and its products and markets and monitors the total scene continuously to highlight causes and effects.

In general the information available to management is not adequate to the decisions that have to be made.

The late Alfred P. Sloan, Junior, for many years Chief Executive of General Motors, made the point that the ever changing market and ever changing product could break any business unless it was prepared for change.

3.7   The marketing organisation

The marketing organisation can vary according to the product lines, the sales volume, the markets and the size of the company.

In marketing in particular a company cannot afford to be indeterminate in its policies and objectives. It must be clear-sighted on its capabilities and its limitations and it must plan to realise its potential. It must be aware of the particular marketing skills demanded by the products and the markets and it must be specific on the achievements expected from the marketing organisation. These are some of the considerations that will influence management in deciding the organisation that is required.

The various activities have to be classified and their importance to the company evaluated.

3.7.1   The sales activity

This is one of the first considerations. The leading question is
how does the company propose to maintain and increase its
share of the market. Will it rely upon a strong sales force or
will advertising be the key factor supported by a number of
sales representatives. Alternatively will the company sell
mainly through distributors supported by a small sales force.
If the company operates in export markets it may decide to
sell through agents or distributors or to establish a sales force.
Conditions can vary and also policies. One well-known British
company had an extensive export market for its product. It
was a long established policy to sell to industrial users only
and to sell through its own sales organisation. Establishing
sales organisations in the major export countries was an expensive undertaking but the managing director decided that
every effort should be made to honour the dead and the
policies they had introduced albeit in a very different environment. The objective was achieved economically by the company acting as sales agents for other British companies in the
export territories.

3.7.2   Sales administration office

The marketing division will most likely receive and process
all sales orders, fix selling price, submit quotations to customers, check that orders are executed by the due dates, deal
with customers complaints, prepare sales invoices and maintain essential records. Many companies find it convenient and
efficient to centralise these activities in a sales office, or sales
administration office, under the supervision of a sales office
manager. In any event these duties require consideration in
deciding the organisation.

3.7.3   Marketing intelligence

It is generally essential in an organisation of any size to have
an information centre that collects and interprets the facts

and figures required by management to plan, direct and control the marketing operation. The centre would maintain the essential statistics from internal records and would classify and interpret data obtained from outside sources and from the sales force. It would, for example, analyse company sales by products and markets and share of the markets. It would obtain economic reports from established sources. It would be largely involved in providing information for long term planning and annual budgeting. It is not unusual to have these activities controlled by an economist/statistician. Companies may have different views on the organisation of these activities but they are essential in some degree in every company. In the large company the intelligence section, by whatever title, is directly responsible to the managing director.

3.7.4   Services

Two kinds of servicing have to be recognised: there is the after-sales service to maintain the article in good working order and there is the technical service that provides information and guidance to customers on the application of the product to their particular conditions.

After-sales service is undertaken in several ways. A company may appoint outside firms to do it for them or the demands may be so small that an engineer may be sent as required. If the company undertakes servicing on a large scale there is usually a service department under a service manager.

Technical services can be very important in connection with certain products. Well organised, these can provide a competitive edge; they can establish good customer relations, provide new applications for existing products and even on occasions be the means of introducing new products. A progressive company achieved all of these through its technical services department.

3.7.5   Transport

The first requirement is to operate as economically as

possible. Companies vary in their practise. Come companies operate through outside contractors, others undertake their own transport. Sometimes a company may combine both to operate economically. Where a company operates its own fleet there will almost certainly be a transport manager in charge. Some of the larger companies employ a transport manager where outside contractors are used as the work involves considerable organisation to give service to customers and to keep costs down. A number of considerations arise in deciding transport policy. The transport manager will probably be responsible to the sales office manager, or sometimes to the marketing director.

3.7.6 Warehousing

The warehousing of finished goods is generally a function of marketing. Dependent upon the size of the company the warehouse will probably be controlled by a warehouse manager. Where a company has warehouses, or depots, located in several districts then it is usual to have a warehouse, or depot, manager. The warehouse manager may be directly responsible to the marketing director or to the sales office manager.

3.7.7 Centralisation

Where a company has several factories at different locations and making different products each factory may be given full autonomy within wide limits. Each may have its own design and development section, its own sales force for its particular products and so on and be subject to the minimum control from head office.

One company with eight factories operated in this manner. Each factory was managed by a local director. The presentation of statements was standardised throughout the company and monthly profit and loss statements in standard form had to be submitted by each factory to head office. Once a year each factory submitted an annual budget together with its long-term planning proposals and the capital commitments involved to head office by a given date. These were sanctioned by the board of directors in due course or modifications agreed upon.

Every factory made a satisfactory profit on the capital investment. But over a period of some three years there were signs, first at one factory and then at another, that the company was losing out against competition although profit was being maintained. The managing director expressed this view at meetings with the factory directors but as there was no general agreement nothing was decided.

Eventually and without persuasion the factory directors reached the same conclusion and the sales forces were centralised under a sales director recruited from outside. After six months it was confirmed that the company had been lagging behind certain leading competitors and it was only an expanding market demand for the several product lines that had protected the sales and the profit.

Many companies have found that decentralised selling activities do not provide the best results.

3.7.8   Summary

Creating the right organisation is a management function. The requirements of the organisation must be clearly defined and it must be based on tomorrow as distinct from today. No two business concerns are alike. The ideas and outlook of management, the type of business and the capabilities of the personnel will all influence the type of organisation. There are no set rules for creating the right organisation but there are guidelines which can aid management decisions.

Figure 3.1 is an example of the marketing organisation of a fairly large company.

3.8   Marketing decisions

Some of the most important and far reaching decisions that a company has to make are in the marketing field; products, markets, volume of sales and selling prices, for example. Most

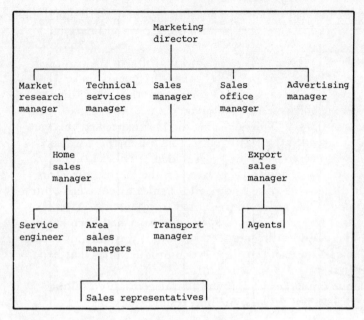

Figure 3.1   Marketing organisation

of the entrepreneurial considerations of a company lie in this field. In this field in particular a company has to be positive and clearsighted in its policies and objectives. The underlying complexity of operating a business is that products do not last; all have a life cycle, some short and others long. Figure 3.2 illustrates a product life cycle. There are five stages in the cycle:

Introduction: When the product is first introduced the sales are minimal.

Growth: The sales curve begins to show a steep rise.

Maturity: Growth continues but at a reducing rate.

Saturation: Sales reach a peak and remain there for a period.

Decline: Sales start to show a steady decline as the product is displaced by better products or substitutes.

Advertising can sometimes prolong the life of the product.

The market is lost to a company sooner or later through better

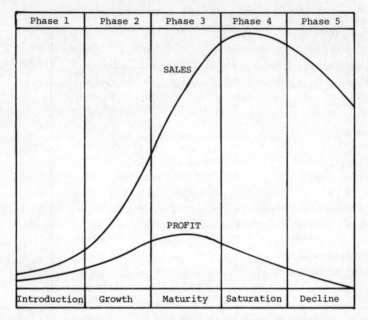

Figure 3.2   Break-even chart

products or substitutes unless it is geared to change. The
length of a product cycle is generally governed by the rate of
technical change and competition.

A company has to observe the activities of competitors but
it has also to intensify its knowledge of technical and scientific developments. Product development is the key to the
situation.

The type of product decides what design and development
means to a company. Many companies have operated in the
same product field for a number of years introducing new
models to the market periodically. This is true of many
products, for example, cars, washing machines and refrigerators to mention only a few. Companies operating in this
category have at least the advantage of knowing their product field and can develop and advance their technology on
positive lines.

There are many companies that operate in a different environment in that their products are generally displaced by

substitutes which may have no relationship to the originals, for example, plastic pipes displacing cast iron. Companies in these circumstances have to develop a field of interest and the technology associated with it in the absence of a definite product line. There are companies, for example, whose interests lie in communications or in the field of electronics or chemicals and their advanced technology earns for them a leading position in the market.

Every company is faced with the task of anticipating and preparing for change to protect and promote its sources of income. It must be reasonably aware of the lead time permitted to it for developing new models or new products by knowing the approximate life cycle of its existing products.

A company must avoid a product gap to avoid a gap in the sales income. If it waits until a product shows signs of decline before it produces a replacement it is in a weak sales position unless it can increase the sales of its other products to compensate.

There are also many factors and decisions involved in planning a development programme and some companies through experience and circumstances have developed a product philosophy as referred to below.

In marketing decisions the accent is on how to obtain and interpret better data. The need is for planned and methodical product and market research which simply means being fully informed on the market situation. Better informed is one of the frontiers of better management.

3.9 Product philosophy

A product philosophy usually results in greater objectivity and the closer coordination of all the activities associated with product development. It generally results in a high degree of sophistication relative to products and markets.

One major European company has been operating through a well developed product philosophy for many years and most successfully. It operates through a product committee that represents all major components of the company. The purpose of the committee is to review and coordinate all product actions.

The objectives of the company are to design, develop, manufacture and sell a range of products covering all major segments of the market, and to achieve the highest standards of quality that the selling prices and the cost objectives will permit. The primary objectives of the committee is to ensure a steady flow of new products that will replace the existing products without any sales gap. It appreciates that a company that loses its initiative loses its place in the markets.

Some companies develop annual budgets three to five years ahead to monitor product replacement and sales. Before a new product is approved the company will be satisfied that it provides a reasonable profit as well as continuity. But until the product mix can be viewed on a time and quantity basis as in a series of annual budgets a company cannot be sure that its sales income is protected. One of the principal objectives of preparing annual budgets for a period of years is to satisfy the company that its sales will be maintained through its products and its markets. Projecting the products and the sales are not sufficient, however, without taking account of the end product which is profit and it is for this reason that long-term budgets and not simply sales forecasts must be developed.

It is not expected that the profit forecasts will be strictly accurate but they must be indicative. The object is to ensure that the profit trends in relation to sales are maintained.

4 Factors that Influence a Sales Forecast

The market demand for a product can be influenced by many factors — some controllable and others uncontrollable. It follows that these same factors influence the accuracy of a sales forecast. A sales forecast may not be strictly accurate but if not on the bull's eye it must at least be on the target. A forecast backed by experience, a fact-finding approach and sound judgement can generally be close enough for most purposes.

Sales forecasting can be broadly considered from three aspects: the industry in which the company operates, the standing of the company within the industry and external or environmental factors.

It is important to evaluate the prospects of the industry and in particular to establish if the product has a growth potential or if the demand is static or declining. A stable demand is not unusual for certain basic products. But a declining demand can be a danger signal. Other important factors are the general efficiency of the industry, the rate of technological development, the average profits on the investment and the ease or difficulty with which new companies are able to break into the industry.

If the product shows a growth potential then the first requirement is satisfied. If the profit margins are good the likelihood of other companies entering the industry has to be considered. This will depend on the general efficiency of the industry and on the size of the capital investment.

It would be difficult for a new company to enter the motor car industry where efficiency is high and the capital investment colossal. But new companies do enter established industries and intensify the competition.

A large manufacturing company with substantial financial resources and technologically advanced in product design and production processes decided to extend its range of products. It looked at some of the long established and sheltered industries that showed good profit earnings and appeared to be outdated in technology and methods. One industry was selected but just before the go-ahead the product design division reported that there was no way round the patents held by the leading companies and the project had to be abandoned.

4.1   The general approach

The initial step is to forecast the total market demand for the product. If this proves difficult the alternative is to forecast the total sales of the industry. If the industry is represented by a trade association total sales figures are generally available. The forecast will take into account the probable rate of sales expansion and the competition, if any, from alternative products.

The second step is to forecast the company's share of the market. Here careful account has to be taken of existing competition based on competitor profiles and marketing intelligence. If a long-term sales forecast is being prepared then the possibility of new companies entering the industry may be a consideration. In an annual sales forecast this is not an immediate consideration.

The third step is to identify and relate changes in the environment — social, economic and political — to the total sales of the industry and company sales. The environmental factors largely condition the climate for business operation — good trading prospects or bad. These factors are the least controllable. The general trading prospects can have a major impact on an annual sales forecast, but have little significance in a long-term forecast.

In essence, therefore, sales forecasting has initially to determine the sales prospects of the industry and then to decide what constraints, if any, are likely to be imposed by the environmental conditions and their effect on total market demand. These factors have then to be related to company sales.

A knowledge of what is going on in an industry can generally be established by market research, marketing intelligence and/or trade associations. These industrial aspects constitute the more controllable factors of market demand. The external factors that influence the general trading conditions have usually to be obtained from outside sources.

A sales forecast for an annual sales budget is normally concerned with

1   Total sales for the industry, or total market demand, analysed by products and markets.
2   Company share in total and analysed by products and markets.

The forecast may then have to be adjusted up or down according to the trading prospects indicated by the probable impact of external factors.

4.2   Forecasting procedures

The period covered by the forecast has to be defined. This can be important as certain factors having a major impact on an annual forecast, e.g. the trading prospects, may have little significance in a long-term forecast.

The products and the markets should be clearly described. Wherever practical the forecast should state quantities as well as values for each product or product line. Markets should have a reference to geographical areas.

Market demand may be for the whole market or it may be analysed by segments. One company analyses the demand in the domestic market by industries and in total. The export demand is analysed by countries.

Some companies confine their sales forecast to major products and major markets; other products and markets are covered by sales estimates based on a statistical analysis of actual sales.

Preparatory to preparing a sales forecast it is generally the practice to analyse actual sales for a previous period, probably three years or more. Sales are analysed by products and markets in financial terms and also by quantities wherever feasible. These figures showing company share of the markets by products are compared with the total market demand shown in the same market. The objective is to identify trends in total market demands and in company share. These trends are projected to provide a sales forecast. Some companies attach great importance to these trends, particularly in their application to short-term forecasts of, say, a year. Whatever value an analysis of past sales may have it cannot be ignored in a forecasting procedure.

Monthly sales forecasts are based on an analysis of previous sales and trends supplemented or modified in the light of current information. If a company operates in an industry where demand is stable an analysis of past sales can provide a useful and reliable basis for sales forecasting. Alternatively if the industry is expanding its sales and the rate of technological development is high then a company must not place too much reliance on past sales and must seek guidance from several sources.

Data from several sources are generally used to project sales forecasts including:

1   Analysis of past sales as already mentioned.
2   Analysis of competitive and complementary industries.
3   Outside services.
4   Field information and estimates.

4.3   Analysis of competitive and complementary industries

A factor that cannot be overlooked in forecasting is the competitive industries and their growth trend and relative positions. A forecast of sales of man-made fibres must take into account the sales demand for the competing natural fibres.

The feeders or consumers of a product line can provide

valuable indicators, e.g. the motor car industry as a guide to steel, glass and instrument manufacturers, and the construction industry as a guide to steel, cement and building plant.

4.3.1   Outside services

Developments within the industry and other factors that can influence total sales and company share of the market should be indicated by market research and marketing intelligence. In general companies are not unduly worried about industrial matters as they have several sources for obtaining information. Most companies, however, do like to know what competitors are doing and this information is not readily available. What worries many companies and induces them to use outside services in one form or another is the effect of external factors on the total sales of the industry. This can be an elusive factor.

Information on external conditions and their effect on business can be obtained from published material. Government departments, banks and private sources all publish information that can be useful. Trade associations can also supply information on external conditions and their probable effect on the industry. International companies in particular are concerned about conditions in world markets and use outside sources to supplement their own intelligence systems.

4.3.2   Field information and estimates

Great reliance is placed on information from the field by a number of companies. This is justifiable where the sales representatives are competent and well trained, knowing the class of information required, how it can be obtained and how it should be interpreted and reported.

A company has to find an answer to the question what are the prospects for the industry and how will these be affected by economic and other external factors. The prospects for the industry will normally be established through field in-

formation and the trade association publications. Information
on economic and other external factors will be obtained
through publications and/or private sources.

4.4   A practical example

One successful company prepares its annual forecast on the
basis of:
1   An analysis of sales for three years showing total demand
    for each major market and company share.
2   An economic report on the domestic market and on im-
    portant export markets.
3   A sales forecast from each area sales manager giving his
    edited version of a sales forecast from each representative.
4   A sales forecast from each of its sales agents abroad.
The home sales manager and the export manager have to submit edited sales forecasts to the marketing director for their
respective areas. Once these are approved by the marketing
director they are submitted to the board of directors or to the
budget committee.

It is a rule of the company that a budget should not be
changed without prior consultation with the person who
prepared it. The area sales manager discusses any differences
with his representatives and the home sales manager with his
area sales managers. It is clearly understood by all from the
sales representatives to the marketing director that sales forecasts impose responsibilities and accountability for performance.

The company is product-market orientated with a carefully
planned and well organised product development programme
There is a product development committee representing
design, manufacture and marketing that meets monthly to
review and make recommendations on products and activities.
The company is usually ahead of competition in new designs
and on occasions has been known to delay launching a new
product as the existing product is still the leader in the field.

Sales performance is under constant review, particularly
the market share, to ensure that the company is maintaining
its competitive position. Sales forecasts are taken very

seriously and accurate forecasts are expected. Area sales managers are advised of the trading prospects for the ensuing year and are responsible for collecting all other information required to submit the annual sales budget. Records are maintained at each branch to show sales for the previous three years. Customers are classified in one of four categories according to the value of their annual purchases. Representatives are supplied with customer sales record cards for all the top categories A and B. The record card shows quarterly sales for four periods and the most recent sales monthly up to a period of three months. Prior to preparing his annual forecast the representative is expected to call on each A and B customer and to summarise his findings on the sales card for the customer. The minimum information required is (a) how does the customer regard the prospects for his business in the following year, will sales increase, remain fairly stable or decrease and (b) how does he regard the standing of the company on product, price, delivery and service and how will this affect the share of his orders.

In finalising his annual sales forecast the sales representative has to show sales for category A in total and subdivided by products showing quantities and values. He does the same for category B and for categories C and D, the latter being entirely an estimate without reference to customers. Each sales representative has a discussion with the area sales manager when the forecast is accepted or amended by agreement. The area sales manager submits his annual forecast for his area to the sales manager in the standard form used by the sales representatives. If the sales manager accepts the forecasts from each area manager these are combined in the standard form and submitted to the marketing director. Any disagreement is discussed between the sales manager and the area manager to arrive at an acceptable conclusion.

The sales forecast for export sales is equally thorough. In some countries the company has established sales offices under the control of sales managers; in other countries sales representation operates through agents. Sales forecasts have to be submitted to the export manager by the sales managers and agents and these are carefully vetted before acceptance.

All sales forecasts are presented to the budget committee by the marketing director.

4.5   The art of forecasting

The art of forecasting stems from a number of factors. The first and most important is top management involvement. Establishing the sources for comprehensive and reliable information inside and outside of the company is essential. Analysing and interpreting the information to determine the facts and to establish meaningful patterns to guide decisions requires skill and experience and this is a critical factor in accurate forecasting.

Forecasting is still an under-developed procedure. The problems of fact finding and decision-making will not be eliminated but more efficient techniques will be progressively developed for dealing with them. The most critical factor is to decide the actions to be taken in the light of the facts presented. Decision-making is in the end a matter of personal and informed judgement with, at best, the risk narrowed down to a few alternatives.

There are few things simple in forecasting. The statistical analysis of previous sales to determine the trends is practised by most companies but this is a skilled operation. In analysing past sales it is necessary to identify secular, cyclical, seasonal and random trends. Random trends, being irregular and unpredictable, have to be identified and eliminated to enable the other trends to be ascertained. The secular or long-term trend indicates the growth trend in the sales of a product over an extended period. The cyclical trend indicates the effect of general business conditions on sales. Monthly figures are really more useful for this purpose and the influence of secular and seasonal trends have to be eliminated to establish the cyclical trend.

Haivng established these trends it is necessary to find out if anything has occurred or might occur to disturb them. The first check is to see if the sales of any product are likely to decline without any compensatory increase in other products. Another check usually less obvious is to establish if competition is likely to change. National boundaries are fast disappearing with the results that markets are extending and also the competition. Products that were previously regarded as sinecures for the domestic market are now facing outside challenges. This can seriously affect the sales of a company unless, of course, it too has extended its sales boundaries.

These are only two of the many factors that require consideration in sales forecasting.

Forecasting that is effectively organised imposes a discipline; it demands the utmost accuracy and reliability and it allocates responsibility with accountability for performance. Where top management is actively and closely involved and makes this involvement apparent throughout the organisation then highly efficient procedures can be established. In the ultimate forecasting procedures, good or ineffective, stem directly from top management. And there are few things more important in a business than reliable sales forecasts.

4.6 Summary

The future is uncertain and forecasting can never be an exact science. The sales of a product are influenced by the interaction of a number of factors. If the major factors can be identified and their effects clearly understood then better forecasting will result. However if there are no certainties in forecasting it can at least provide safeguards if it is undertaken properly and effectively.

Most companies probably rely on a combination of forecasting and prediction to project their sales forecasts. Statistical forecasting may be described as projecting the past into the future. There are many industries where product demand is relatively stable and changes, if any, are insignificant and gradual. In these cases statistical forecasting serves their purposes.

Probably in the majority of industries reliance is based on statistical forecasting with certain adjustments to take account of changes and new factors arising that may affect product sales. These adjustments are based on predictions and may stem from introducing a new product, extending the market, or increased competition from new competitors.

In the background, of course, there is always the question of the general trading prospects and how these will affect product demand. Whatever the forecasting procedure may be, good or bad trading conditions can affect it and have to be taken into account. Information for forecasting can be obtained from three sources: (a) the sales records of the business and from them the preparation of a statistical forecast; (b) what is happening within the industry and a prediction of the effect of changes or new factors on product sales; (c) the external factors influencing the trading position and their likely effect on market and sales.

There is another factor that has to be considered and that is the efficiency of the marketing activity. A vigorous marketing policy can influence sales and this factor must be taken into account in forecasting. It follows too that a company that is the leader in the field can forecast with more conviction and reliability than a company further down the scale. Forecasting sales in conditions that are generally complex and almost infinitely variable requires skill, knowledge and experience coupled with informed judgement of a high order. What the sales figures show and what the industry is doing can be obtained through a statistical forecast and marketing intelligence largely gleaned from the field force; the economic environment in which the business has to operate will frequently be determined from outside sources. Some large companies employ economists to provide guidance on economic and environmental conditions. But the interaction of all the factors that can affect the results have to be evaluated.

A sales forecast has to be translated into a sales budget and here a number of factors have to be taken into consideration as mentioned later.

5 Price-fixing and the Considerations Involved

A selling price reflects a number of factors that are generally summed up in what the market is prepared to pay. Prices may not be identical but are generally relative and the company that demands a higher price for its product will have to justify it.

Products can be broadly classified as standard and non-standard from the view-point of selling price procedure; the business that manufactures standard products generally issues price lists whereas orders for non-standard products are normally placed against quotations.

Price-fixing is a matter of policy and it is important that all the relevant factors are identified and taken into account in framing the policy. A company must have a close understanding of the markets, the industry in which it operates, total market demand for the product and its market standing in relation to competitors. A knowledge of how selling prices tend to be fixed within the industry is another important factor. A profit objective is essential in formulating policy.

One of the factors that influences price is product cost — not the cost of the individual manufacturer but of the industry as a whole. It has to be recognised, however, that in some industries there is one company that is recognised as the leader and which takes the initiative in price changes which other companies tend to follow. A product cost is not a simple fact; it is a summary of basic costs and volume costs as well as other factors. Cost comprises many items — some that are measurable in terms of the product and some that are arbitrary, some that are fixed and some that are variable. Opinions can enter into the make-up of costs and produce different answers.

The factors that basically decide the manufacturing cost of a product are design and development (which determine the materials content and work content) and volume (which determines the amount to be charged per unit for fixed costs). Expressed in general terms fixed costs per unit vary with volume, the greater the volume the lower the cost. In contrast variable costs tend to be fixed in relation to volume.

A product may have all the basic characteristics to compete successfully, i.e. be well designed to satisfy the standards of the market and economical to produce but unless the business operates at or above the production level common throughout the industry it will be in a weak competitive position to obtain an adequate selling price.

In introducing a new product or an improved design of an existing product some companies think in terms of the selling price bracket before the project starts. Their objective is to fix the desirable cost objective and to provide the best possible value to the customer within its limitation.

Some of the factors that have to be considered are:

1   Profit policy related to price-fixing.
2   The effect of volume on profit.
3   Fixing selling prices by following the general practice of the industry.
4   Conventional costs as a guide to selling prices.
5   The application of marginal costs in terms of contribution.
6   Other factors that can influence selling prices.

5.1   Profit policy

Some of the leading companies aim at a specific return on the capital investment with due regard to volume of sales and selling prices. What constitutes the capital investment is not always a simple matter to define and opinions differ. One method that is simple to apply is to take the gross assets as representing the capital employed in the business.

Generally companies have justifiable reasons for fixing the minimum return expected on capital employed. Probably the rate of return is based on previous performance with every reason to expect that this can be maintained. Volume is, of course, an important factor in fixing selling prices, as it pinpoints the fixed costs that will be charged to the product in a conventional costing system.

One leading company has for years based its selling price on an average operating capacity of 80 per cent and a minimum return of 15 per cent on capital employed. In operating this procedure a company has to determine the number of units that can be produced at varying levels of capacity and the costs appropriate to each level. If, for example, the total capacity of the plant is 100,000 units in a period and the normal operating capacity is 80 per cent then this will be represented by 80,000 units. If each unit costs £100 then the total cost will be £8,000,000. The next point to be determined is the rate of return that can normally be expected in relation to the capital employed. If the capital employed is £5,000,000 and the rate of return is 20 per cent then the anticipated profit would be £1,000,000.

The mark up on cost would be 12½ per cent:

	Total	Per unit
Number of units	80,000	–
Total cost	£8,000,000	£100.0
Profit	£1,000,000	£12.5
Total sales	£9,000,000	£112.5

There are three factors involved in this procedure: first the operating capacity and the number of units this represents, second the costs appropriate to this level of capacity and third the mark up on cost for profit. Volume of sales is the basis used for calculating cost and selling price but price can influence sales. It is particularly important that a company should analyse the demand and the effects of competition and economic conditions to ensure that the selling price will generate the anticipated volume of output.

Product costs can provide guide lines for fixing selling prices. They can measure the profitability of a selling price but they cannot give any guide to the mark up on costs to arrive at selling price.

5.2   The effect of volume on profit

If costs varied directly in proportion to variations in volume, this in itself would have a marked effect on profit. Volume assumes greater importance because costs cannot be reduced in proportion to a reduction in volume nor will they increase to the same extent as volume increases because of the element of fixed and partly variable costs. In the short term few expenses are variable whereas in the long term few are fixed. Production materials are a typical directly variable cost. Direct labour cost was generally classed as variable but changes in the conditions of employment and the development of more advanced production techniques have tended to place it in the category of a partly variable cost. The stage is being reached in some industries where volume can change to quite an extent without a change in costs, other than production materials.

Of all the factors that can influence costs, volume is probably the least controllable being affected to a large extent and very quickly by fluctuations in the order intake, particularly with non-standard products where there is no possibility of making for stock to maintain production at a constant level. Reference has been made previously to a break-even chart which is a simple device for demonstrating profit/ volume relationships and the effect of changes in costs, volume and other factors such as selling prices.

Every company should accumulate data to show its volume operation in relation to the total production capacity of the plant. A study of the volume performance for the previous three years should give a fair indication of the standard or normal activity in most cases. If the company has made a satisfactory profit while operating at this level then product costs developed on this basis should provide the guidelines for fixing selling prices.

A company manufacturing non-standard products increased its output in real value every year for several years and its overheads, expressed as a rate per hour, steadily dropped. New overhead rates were calculated each year and used in the calculation of product costs and selling prices with the result that all the benefits of increased volume were passed on to the customer. When the significance of this procedure became apparent the company adopted a production level of 80 per cent for product costing and price-fixing, an arrangement that proved more profitable to the company and satisfactory to the customer. This is an unusual case inasmuch as the up-swing in volume each year did not provide a normal. The volume operations of most companies tend to be more consistent and a normal volume can generally be identified.

Most companies will be operating at a capacity level on average to earn a viable profit. The more efficient companies, market leaders in particular, will be earning a surplus profit at their operating level and will adopt a lower level of capacity for product costing and price-fixing. Conversely the marginal producer operating at a level not far removed from the break-even point may find that its product costs have to be projected at a higher than normal volume level to calculate competitive selling prices.

The business that produces standard products may use its product costs as a measure of its ability to meet the market price rather than as a means of fixing selling price.

The implications of volume and its effect on product costs have to be understood. Volume is only one of several factors that can influence product cost. Product cost is only one of many factors that can influence selling price so at best costs provide essential guidelines only.

5.3   Price-fixing in the industry

Following the leaders is probably the oldest practice in fixing selling prices. In some industries it is quite usual for members to follow a system of uniform costing which provides at least a rational basis for price-fixing.

A company may decide to fix its prices at a lower level than the leaders and to maintain this differential as prices increase. The important factor is that the company does not rely on its own costs for fixing selling prices, nor does it generally determine the point at which an increase in selling price is justified.

5.4   Absorption costing

Absorption costing, or as it is sometimes termed full costing is used by very many companies as a basis for price-fixing. Critics of absorption costing contend that the arbitrary allocation of overheads which is inherent in this system can lead to unreliable product costs.

The cost of a product under absorption costing would probably be detailed as follows:

	£
Materials cost Factory operating costs	
SUB-TOTAL	
Selling costs Technical costs Administration costs Distribution cost	
TOTAL COST	

Some of the most powerful companies and many of the more efficient ones cost their products through absorption costing and any that do not show a net profit are quickly eliminated. There are also companies that are not strong enough financially to follow this procedure. They cling to products that do not show a profit but which make a contribution to fixed costs and thereby improve the profit position. Their difficulty is that they do not have new products to displace the marginal products.

In several of the industries that are represented by trade associations it is customary to develop uniform costing systems particular to the industry. Since the uniform costing system is applied by all members to establish product costs it tends to ensure that the selling prices related to these costs are soundly based to create fair competition. As a general rule the uniform costing systems are based on absorption costing.

In looking at alternative costing systems which undoubtedly have particular merit in special circumstances, for example marginal costing or direct costing, the hard fact has to be recognised that the profit and loss statement is the ultimate measure of business performance and it is the net profit that counts.

In the efficient company the business is profit-orientated and every product has to show a profit and the aggregate of profits has to provide not less than a quoted figure on the assets or capital employed. In short the selling price has to exceed the full cost of the product.

5.5   Marginal costing

Marginal costs can be established through the conventional costing system based on absorption costing.

The idea behind marginal costing is that the fixed expenses have to be met by the current volume of output and if the output can be increased the only additional cost incurred is the variable or 'out of pocket' costs. If the additional output can be sold at a price that covers the variable costs plus a contribution to fixed costs then the total profits of the business can be increased.

No company should be in business to earn marginal profits or to regularly produce a product that only earns a marginal profit. There can be occasions, however, when a business may find it expedient and profitable to sell a product in a marginal price market or to make a product with a marginal profit as a temporary measure to utilise surplus capacity.

This seemingly innocuous process of marginal costing has to be closely watched as it can lead to manufacturing the wrong product lines.

A fairly large chemical company operated five factories in various parts of the country each manufacturing a different chemical on a continuous production process with plant specially designed for the purpose. Head office, the marketing division and the technical division were centrally located away from the factories.

One of the products was slightly affected by seasonal demand and it was customary for the company to accept contracts from abroad to maximize production output.

Again it had been the practice of the company to accept marginal selling prices. The managing director was uneasy on the basis adopted to fix the marginal selling prices and he asked consultants to examine the procedure.

It transpired that the costs of operating head office and the marketing and technical divisions were allocated to the factories on an arbitrary basis. The consultants eliminated these costs as a means of assessing the costs directly incurred by the particular factory concerned. It then examined the break-down of the factory costs as between fixed and variable expenses and reached the conclusion that all the costs were virtually fixed with the exception of production materials.

The consultants agreed with the conclusions reached by the accountants of the company that factory costs, excepting materials, were fixed and that the costs of the head office and the other divisions were also fixed. The consultants reported that the accounting application was correct but to sell a product at *less* than production cost was commercially unsound. They advised that the selling price should be based on production cost plus a mark up for profit, plus, of course, any shipping charges that would be incurred and the commission payable to the sales agent abroad. This procedure was adopted and was completely successful.

The real test of marginal pricing does not rest on the accounting procedure but is judged by commercial standards.

The foregoing remarks have considered the basis of establishing marginal costs through the conventional costing procedures. There are also marginal costing systems that differ in principle from conventional costing in that they exclude fixed expenses in calculating the product cost. These will be considered later under management accounting.

5.6   Other factors

Price by itself will not necessarily influence the sales of a product — quality, style, brand acceptance, service and availability of the product can also be determining factors. These factors can give a company a competitive edge that will not only influence sales but can often be reflected in a higher selling price.

Quality and style have to be acceptable to the customer; if not the manufacturer may have to charge a lower price to obtain sales. Where quality and style are obviously superior this can justify a higher selling price probably at no added cost to the manufacturer as it does not follow that the best designed product is the most expensive. Experience shows that a well designed product gives due attention to economy as well as quality.

Brand acceptance can influence sales and selling prices. The product has to be good and widely advertised to warrant acceptance.

Service may be simply the attention that is given to executing orders or it may be the reliability of the company in honouring delivery dates. Industrial buyers in particular attach great importance to reliable deliveries of articles that enter into their products as delays in production can be expensive.

Some companies, dependent upon the product, provide a valuable technical service to customers at no cost and this undoubtedly influences sales. Then there is the after-sales service to correct faults or to service the equipment. The efficiency of this service can influence the sales of the product.

The availability of a product can have a marked effect on volume of sales. If the supermarket does not have the brand the housewife requires she will generally select another brand. Industrial users may have their preferred suppliers but if they have to wait more than a few weeks for delivery they will probably look elsewhere for a quicker supply. This applies particularly when increased demands lead to extended delivery dates.

The factors that can influence sales and selling prices are so numerous that guide lines cannot be established to meet every situation. Efficient companies, particularly the leaders in their respective fields, appear to fix selling prices on a straightforward basis. First, every product has to produce a net profit or it is replaced. Secondly, there is the principle of a reasonable return on the capital investment projected against the sales obtainable at a certain level of operating capacity. Selling price is based on absorption costing, total cost, with a mark up to realise the desired return on investment. One very large and efficient company aims at a return of 15-20 per cent on its investment against an operating capacity of 80 per cent.

The efficiency of a company has a bearing on its price-fixing procedure. Companies below the leaders can be faced frequently with a complex pricing situation and the degree of complexity increases as efficiency drops to the marginal level. The less efficient companies cannot look at every product in terms of net profit but have to identify the products that provide the best contribution.

The maximisation of profit is not always regarded in a favourable light. The comments of some of the chief executives of outstanding companies in this connection are interesting. Invariably these executives believe in the maximisation of profit. They are not looking for easy profit. They believe that profit is the result of giving the best possible value to the customer within the limits of the selling price. Their policy is to maximise value and through it to maximise profit. Their products provide convincing evidence of this policy.

6 The Sales Budget

The sales forecast provides the foundation for the sales budget. The sales budget is generally for one year to coincide with the financial year but it is also important for a company to see its sales volume in terms of products and markets for the next three to five years and this requires in addition longer-term budgeting.

The master budget assesses the prospects of the company for the ensuing year in terms of sales and profit. This assessment has to take into account the trading conditions and the probable effect of competitive, economic, social and political factors.

Strategic planning provides the products, the markets, marketing and distribution channels and the production facilities; it is the purpose of the annual budget to obtain the maximum volume of sales of the right product mix to satisfy the profit aim and to provide a balanced production programme. The budget plan has to find answers to the questions: How should the business operate during the next financial year? What can we hope to achieve? What tactics should we adopt to achieve it?

Undoubtedly the annual budget is the most effective basis for controlling sales and profit. Strategic long-term planning aims at creating the conditions for profitable operation and growth. Long-term sales forecasting aims at ensuring that there are no gaps in the strategic long-term plans and that sales and profit will at least be maintained at the current level. Annual budgeting has for its objective the realisation of sales and profit.

The annual master budget is developed through a sales budget, a production budget and various expense budgets, all of which are translated into a profit budget.

6.1   Preparing the sales budget

It is generally the responsibility of the marketing director to translate the annual sales forecast into a sales budget. In the large company he may have the assistance of statisticians and economists to forecast and predict the total market demand for each product in the various markets and the trading conditions that are likely to prevail during the period of the budget. But in the final analysis it is usually the responsibility of the director to determine share of the market for each product.

The first consideration is to ensure that the information provided by the forecast is relevant, comprehensive and complete. In general the forecast should be based on an analysis of past experience, forecasts from the field and a forecast of general business conditions. The tendency towards growth or decline of a product is always present and where sales figures for the industry are available it is useful to check company sales against industry sales. This also provides the company with a reference for checking its share of the markets.

The sales forecast should provide the following information as a minimum requirement:

1   *Sales by product lines.* Where more than a single product is produced then sales should preferably be shown in quantity as well as value to guide the preparation of the production budget.

2   *Sales by territories.* This is important to ensure that the requirements and conditions of each territory have been studied and that the sales representation is adequate.

3   *Sales by customer classes.* Customers are classified into groups according to the total annual sales. This is essential where trade discounts vary by category. The

classification may take the form of wholesalers, retailers, supermarkets, chain stores, etc, when the product is sold at different prices.

4 *Statistical analysis of previous sales.* This analysis should show the same information as indicated above for comparison purposes.

5 *Total sales of the industry and company sales by products and markets.* This information if available can be extremely useful.

The marketing director will compare the sales potential shown by the forecast with previous sales performance by markets and products. Any lack of growth or sales recession in a market or product will obviously require attention. He will have to anticipate the outlook of the board of directors and where the sales budget is likely to run counter to their expectations he must verify the information and have valid reasons for presenting the figures.

After deciding on a tentative sales budget the director will consider what factors, if any, will react against achieving it. This may involve a close look at the marketing organisation and particularly at sales representation. It may be that the sales representation in some territories does not match the sales potential. Providing the board of directors gives authority to recruit the additional sales representatives required, six months of the annual period may well elapse before any benefits are obtainable. If the sales representation applies to countries abroad and sales agents have to be appointed there may be no benefit to the company throughout the budget year. This is one of several factors that can lead to amendments in an otherwise attainable sales budget.

6.2 Sales budget approval

A company has to give careful consideration to the sales budget as the structure of all other budgets is largely conditioned by it. The sales budget may be presented in the first place to the budget committee, which will include the marketing director.

The committee will examine the budget from several view-

points:
1   *Budgeted sales in relation to previous sales performance.*
     The committee will be interested to know if the sales
     budget projects an increase in sales for all markets and
     every product. If sales are static in any market or show-
     ing a reducing trend then explanations will be required.
     The extent of the sales increases will be measured and
     interpreted in terms of the inherent sales growth of the
     product and any shift in share of market. Based on these
     and, perhaps, other considerations the committee may
     submit the budget with their comments for the approval
     of the board of directors or return it to the marketing
     director for further consideration with regard to particu-
     lar aspects.
2   *Sales budget in relation to production capacity.* Market-
     ing and sales executives do not always appreciate that a
     sales budget should provide a balanced production pro-
     gramme and should to a large extent utilise the produc-
     tion capacity. A product mix that is good for a sales
     budget may not provide a balanced production pro-
     gramme and production capacity will not therefore be
     properly or economically utilised. Companies that are
     sophisticated in budgeting appreciate the importance of
     formulating a sales budget that will economically utilise
     production capacity and the marketing director will
     most certainly have consultations with the production
     director. Indeed the budgeting committee will expect
     that general agreement has been reached on this point
     before the sales budget is submitted to them for con-
     sideration.
3   *Increase in inventory.* An increase in sales will almost
     certainly require an increase in inventory and it is
     important to have an indication of the extent of the
     increase. Stocks of raw materials, purchased components,
     work in progress and, perhaps, finished goods will gener-
     ally have to increase in relation to sales.
   Quite often there has to be a compromise between sales
requirements and production capabilities and limitations and
this should be resolved by the joint efforts of the marketing
and production directors before the sales budget is finalised.

Any increase in production capacity involving additional plant to meet an increased sales demand is generally too long term to be achieved in the annual budget period.

Once a sales budget is approved it is in effect a sales programme imposing full responsibility on the marketing division for its achievement. Companies experienced in budgeting may find that they do not always achieve their target but they generally improve their performance.

Budgeting is a complex operation and this is most marked in the preparation of sales budgets. Many of the major decisions in business lie in the marketing area and it is here perhaps more than anywhere that the art of budgeting is most pronounced.

6.3   Long-term budgeting: its purpose and limitations

Consideration has centred on the annual sales budget as a starting point in the budgeting procedure which leads to a profit budget and a projected balance sheet.

The emphasis has been placed on an annual budget because it can be the most effective tool available to management for influencing sales, controlling costs and increasing profit. Although not an ideal standard the fact is that management performance is judged on the results of the annual profit and loss statement and this makes the case for an annual budget. Business is so competitive that some managements virtually hold their positions on an annual lease and the renewal of the lease is conditioned by profit performance.

The great advantage of an annual budget is that it is close to the events and its projections are likely to be more reliable for this reason. Long-term budgeting that extends over a period of two years or more will be less reliable. For one thing it will be less likely to gauge the trading climate — an important factor in budget predictions.

Long-term budgeting has its particular uses and much depends upon what a company hopes to achieve by it. If it is introduced as an extension of annual budgeting in the hope that it will have a direct influence on profit, as is the function of the annual budget, then it will probably fall short of expectations. Long-term budgeting can be applied purposefully and effectively when it is monitoring long-term strategic planning.

Two of the most important considerations in a top management programme are to ensure that there is a regular flow of new products to replace existing products that have passed their peak and that sales are maintained and improved through market share and the development of new markets wherever practicable. There is also the need to ensure that the product profit/sales volume relationship is held at a reasonable and consistent level. What a company must avoid is a sales gap that will reduce sales. This is the aspect that can be monitored by long-term budgeting. Two of the more important considerations in strategic long-term planning are the creation of a product development programme and a marketing programme. These have generally to be considered together as the product must be related to the market and both have to be coordinated from the viewpoint of priorities and completion dates.

6.3.1   A practical example

The policy of a large international company is to sell its products in all major markets and it has established production plants in several countries to further this objective.

Much of its success has been due to its product development programme backed by advanced technology and sophisticated management information systems. At the outline stage of the development of a new product a decision is made on the selling price bracket and this is translated into a desirable cost bracket. The product is designed and developed with this cost objective in view and with the dedicated purpose of providing the maximum value within the cost standards set.

The company has recently made a close study of expanding markets that were previously neglected and its marketing programme incorporates plans for developing them. The company has planned to establish a production plant in one of the markets to be developed.

6.4   Monitoring strategic planning

Many aspects of strategic planning are expressed in the form
of individual projects all of which are coordinated under a
master plan. Every project is tested against selected standards
before it is approved. The development of a new product has
for example to pass the test of sales volume and profit margin
before it is acceptable. Similar standards apply to the development of a new market. Strategic planning must be centred on
creating the conditions for profitable operation and growth.
The efficient and progressive company is aware that this requires an expansion of sales and an assurance that profit
margins of products and market will be held at a satisfactory
level. Maintaining and improving the sales volume requires a
product development programme to ensure that new products
will be available as and when existing products are outdated
and have to be withdrawn.

Other considerations can also arise; there is always the
possibility of extending the markets for the products, there is
the question of updating and probably expanding the production facilities, and there is a need to consider what specific
changes may be required to gear the organisation to the
changing conditions and more exacting competitive demands
that will undoubtedly confront a company in general with
other companies.

A company may be thorough and comprehensive in its
long-term plans. Every project may have been thoroughly
tested as being essential, valid and financially sound. But in
the end the plan largely consists of a series of individual
projects unrelated financially. What is required is a total view,
an assessment of the impact of the projects on the operation
of the business and a measure in periods of time. If corporate
planning is based on a five-year plan then the probable effect
of the planning projects should be evaluated annually for the
five years. The product development programme and marketing programme should provide the basis for evaluating sales in
each of the five years. It should also provide the basis for
assessing the cost of sales each year. The projects relating to
production facilities will provide the guidelines for evaluating
the capital expenditure in each of the five years. In addition

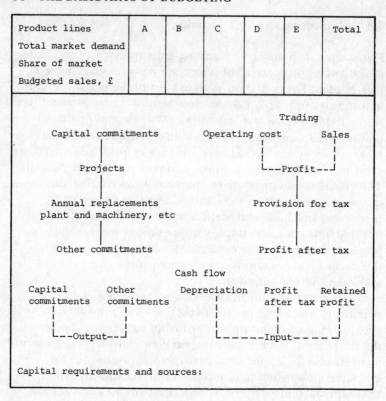

Product lines	A	B	C	D	E	Total
Total market demand						
Share of market						
Budgeted sales, £						

Figure 6.1   Annual budget: basis for long-term budgeting

to the capital or increased revenue expenditure that can arise from product developments, market extensions and the organisation plans other capital expenditure may emerge, for example, financing increased sales and the increase in inventories resulting from the increase in sales.

Summarising the projects contained in the long-term strategic plans and their implications together with the capital expenditure involved is the unique function of long-term budgeting in which the time span will be determined by the futurity of the strategic plans. Where the long-term budgeting exposes weaknesses in the strategic plans then it follows that timely action can be taken to correct the situation and in particular to avoid a gap in sales and consequently profit.

It has to be appreciated that long-term budgets are broadly

structured except for sales income which has to be fully detailed as this is the most important factor to be monitored. Composite cost figures are used to avoid detail; the cost of sales is summarised from the projects for new products to be introduced and from the standard costs of existing products; and the operating costs of the other divisions are based on summary estimates. Figure 6.1 shows a budget that is generally suitable for this purpose together with explanatory notes.

The marketing division is generally responsible for summarising and reporting the sales by products and markets for each year of the budgeting period. This is a logical sequence as this division is generally responsible for providing the sales information for each project, that is the selling price and volume of sales for each new product and each new market. The exercise is to translate the product development programme and the marketing programme into sales for each year of the budgeting period with due regard to the launching date for each new product and the implementation date of any market extension. The budgeted sales of existing products have to take into account the withdrawal dates of outdated products, the latter being decided by the launching dates of replacement products. It can follow in practice, of course, that a replacement product may not be introduced as planned because the current product is holding its place in the market.

6.5 Sales budgeting in perspective

There are two generally recognised systems of sales budgeting and one, if not both, is applied by many companies. Some companies interpret and apply long-term budgeting as an extension of the annual budget, i.e. as a basis for maximising sales and controlling costs and profit. Fewer companies recognise the importance of continually monitoring the probable effects of strategic planning on future sales and profit and the vital importance of long-term budgeting when it is applied with this objective in view.

It is important to recognise that budgeting should impose a discipline. To be fully effective a budget plan must allocate responsibility and accountability for performance. An organisation must not be set the impossible task of implementing a budget that is not factually based or be held responsible for achieving a performance that has not been properly defined. This may be regarded as the limitations of long-term budgeting. After the first year of the budget and certainly after the second year figures can be less reliable and cannot be regarded as a suitable basis for a discipline with accountability for performance.

In fact it is doubtful if any budgeting procedure other than an annual budget can properly be regarded as a discipline imposing responsibility for performance. An annual budget is close to the events and when there is a factual approach based on knowledge, experience, comprehensive information, facts and sound judgement it contains the reliability essential to an acceptable discipline. Disciplines are readily acceptable to the organisation when they are justifiable and attainable with a clear understanding of the purpose, the necessity and the advantages to be obtained and where there is a sense of real participation from top management downwards.

To sum up, the annual budget is the procedure to be adopted to influence sales, costs and profit to the best advantage. The virtue of long-term budgeting is to monitor the results attainable from strategic planning and to inform management of the extent that it fulfils the future needs of the business.

In conclusion it has to be emphasised that the sales budget is the greatest imponderable in the annual budget plan. It has the greatest influence on the prospects of a business but is the least controllable. Thus, every possible effort has to be made to ensure the validity of a sales budget.

6.6   Improving the business

It cannot be concluded from the procedures previously mentioned that all management has to do is to adopt these procedures and all will be well for the company. Much depends upon the substance behind the procedure. A product philosophy, a products development programme and a marketing programme constitute advanced thinking and are generally operated by companies with a long record of outstanding performance and sophisticated in the arts of management. This sophistication has generally stemmed from a close and continuous study of the business and the experience gained over the years. It has largely stemmed from meeting the challenge of new situations.

The majority of companies do not practice these philosophies probably because they do not appreciate their value or have no knowledge of their application. Putting these practices into operation will not produce quick results because of the groundwork involved but will at least put a company on the right lines.

Products, markets and volume of sales normally decide how soundly the business is established and how well it is operating. But all products are outdated sooner or later by competition and the ultimate strength of a business is decided by its ability to match competition and to retain or improve its share of the market. In some companies this is a matter of updating product designs while in others it depends upon the design and development of entirely new products. The right time to introduce a new model or an entirely new product is when the opportunity arises. To update a model or look for a new product when the need arises is the wrong way to run a business.

6.7   Management information systems

Reference has been made previously to marketing information and the value of market research. In recent years some companies have been giving close attention to marketing intelligence which may be described as the systematic collection of relevant information, its analysis and evaluation to establish the facts and the logical grouping of these facts into patterns that may suggest or indicate the shape of future events.

Market research has progressively established itself over the last fifty years but marketing intelligence is a comparatively recent innovation. Market research usually deals with a specific project, for example, a survey for a new product. Marketing intelligence does not focus on particular projects or problems but establishes reliable sources of information relevant to the company's operations and its products and markets and monitors this continuously to measure the probable effect on the business. The objective of marketing intelligence is to forewarn as a means of preventing major problems from arising rather than to examine their implications in retrospect.

H. L. Gantt, one of the pioneers of scientific management, made the statement that it is immoral to decide as a matter of opinion what can be established as a matter of fact. Many companies do not derive the benefits they should obtain from budgeting and other aspects of corporate planning because they do not concentrate enough on establishing the facts.

Many of the big decisions in business will be based on or influenced by the information provided by market research and marketing intelligence and the requirement will increase in volume and complexity. The problems in fact finding will not be eliminated or reduced, but more efficient techniques for dealing with them will be required and will certainly emerge, particularly in the factual interpretation of information.

Many companies extend their information services to the total operations of the business and have a central point for collecting and analysing all information. The processing of information can be an expensive operation involving administration, and experienced analysts and economists and, in the bugger organisation, computer time.

This concept of integrated information services will probably include:

1   *Products and markets:* sales by products and markets and market share.

2   *Competitor profiles:* the strengths and weaknesses of competitors, their resources and competitive strategies — related where possible to products, markets, sales and technology.

3   *New technology:* the rate of technological development, the life span allowed for company products before competition outdates them and the trends in the new technology.

4   *Social and political climate.*

5   *Domestic and overseas business conditions.*

Some large companies employ a number of talented people to provide an integrated information service. The sources of the information are generally a combination of internal information, information obtained from the field through the sales representatives, external information obtained from special sources, general publications and market research projects.

Establishing information for the domestic market can present problems but foreign markets can pose much greater problems. Banks provide a useful service in their economic reports on many countries. The large international companies with factories and offices in many countries can to a large extent collect the necessary information on the spot. One company with more than thirty offices and factories overseas provides a computer link with headquarters.

Futurity and uncertainty are inevitably linked. It is impossible to foresee the future but much can be learned from a study of the past as there is always a semblance of continuity, not perhaps for any one company but certainly for companies as a whole. A company has usually to settle for intelligent guesses but guesses that are based on informed and experienced judgement.

Probability forecasting is gaining acceptance as the best method of forecasting. The forecaster is a skilled statistician. He studies all alternatives and rates the probability of each alternative. Chance occurrences are not overlooked in these considerations. A management informed on probabilities and expectations is better placed to make the right decisions.

The company that aims at progress and growth has to anticipate the future however difficult it may be to project it.

6.8   Marketing cost budget

Reference has been made to the sales budget prepared by the marketing division. In addition this division submits a budget of its operating costs for the year under review.

It is usual to consider expenditure in relation to responsibility and accountability for control. The responsibilities are generally defined in terms of functions and sub-functions and the following classification is fairly common to most companies:

1   The selling function.
2   Advertising and sales promotion.
3   Administration.
4   Information services.
5   Technical services.
6   Transport and shipping.
7   Warehousing.

The next stage is to classify the expenditure under appropriate expense headings, e.g. salaries, wages, commission and travelling expenses. An estimate is then made of the amount to be spent under each heading and the proportion to be allocated to each function or sub-function. The ratio of each expense to total sales can be useful for budgeting expenses and controlling costs.

It is quite common to subdivide the total operating costs of the division into (a) selling costs and (b) distribution costs. One of the reasons for this segregation is that each group has varying characteristics in relation to sales; selling expenses are virtually fixed while distribution costs are fairly elastic.

Some companies like to relate their selling and distribution costs to products to arrive at a total cost for each product. It is generally necessary to deal separately with selling costs and distribution costs as the basis of allocation can be quite different.

Some costs can be directly related to products and these should be charged accordingly; for example the selling costs where the sales activity is organised by product lines. In many cases, however, direct measurement is not possible and costs have to be allocated on an arbitrary basis. In the absence of a better method it is usual to allocate the costs as a percentage of selling price. If the budgeted sales are, say, £1,000,000 and the costs are £100,000 then 10 per cent of the selling price will be charged to the product.

Before applying an arbitrary basis of allocating costs to products it may be necessary to identify costs that are peculiar to markets. It may be for example that certain costs are particular to the domestic market while others are related to export markets. These costs must be segregated and a separate cost to sales ratio established for each market. Costs that are common to both will be related to total sales and a percentage obtained as shown above.

6.9 Summary

The character of the business, what it is and what it should be, is decided by long-term planning. How to make the most of what the business is becomes the province of annual budgeting.

The future is unknown. The uncertainty of the future cannot be wholly eliminated from decision-making. But the difficulty of forecasting does not alter the fact that management must plan for the future. Trends, and probabilities, provide the guidelines. Marketing intelligence and market research provide generalised and specific information on current events. The growth trend of each major product line in each major market, the life cycles of the products, the impact of competition both direct and indirect, the market rating of the products and market shares and technological developments are some of the factors that are under constant review. All of these factors permit a company to see where it stands within the industry and how it is progressing.

A company must take all reasonable steps to establish the facts. It must cultivate the factual approach to decision-making. It must avoid the cardinal sin of accepting as a matter of opinion what can be established as a matter of fact.

7 The Production Function

The economic function of the industrial enterprise is to supply a product that will satisfy market demand and sell at a profit. It is the production function that satisfies this demand by producing the product in the required quantity of the right quality at the right time and at a competitive cost.

The other major functions are a means to this end. The marketing function establishes that there is a market demand for the product; it submits a product specification setting out the requirements of the market; it ensures a large enough share of the market to provide the volume necessary for the product to be made at a competitive cost.

The product design function ensures that the product is in the form most acceptable to the market and is economical to produce. The financial function provides and harnesses the financial resources. But however well these functions perform they are dependent upon the production output for the fulfilment of their objectives.

A competitive manufacturing cost is largely determined by two basic factors — the design of the product and the volume of production. The design determines the material content and work content of a product and the simplicity and ease of manufacture. Volume influences the method of manufacture and the type of facilities that can be used. Other factors are involved but competitive costs demand that a company must be able to match competition in economy and quality of design and volume.

Given the basic essential for profitability, the next consideration is the efficiency of operation. The methods and means of production, the organisation of the total manufacturing function and the established practices and procedures can all have a marked effect on the operating efficiency.

7.1 The types of production

Companies are not identical in their organisation of production but certain types of product tend to be associated with certain methods of production. The two factors that have the greatest influence on the type of production are the product and the volume of sales.

Types of products can be broadly classified as being homogeneous or consisting of an assembly of parts. The product generally establishes the basis of production but volume determines the particular method.

Dependent upon the volume, production may be continuous or intermittent. Large volumes provide an opportunity for continuous production, e.g. process production for the homogeneous product and mass production for the assembly product. Intermittent production generally means batch production or jobbing work.

Process or flow production is the most advanced method and is usually fully automated. The plant is specially designed for the product and cannot generally be adapted for another product. The raw materials are fed in at one end, moved automatically between one production stage and another, and emerge as a finished product. Recording charts are often inserted at strategic points in the plant to measure the flow. This type of manufacture is generally limited in its application to a homogeneous product, for example, chemical, beer and oil refining.

Mass production applies to the assembly type of product manufactured in large quantities. The production of motor cars is the outstanding example. It attempts to simulate process production but falls short because of the nature of the product. It is not, of course, fully automated in terms of the product but only for certain parts and processes. The characteristic of this type of production is that the machines are permanently set up to do a particular operation, or series of operations, thus avoiding delays through tool changes and queuing. It operates on the flow principle and stores are not generally provided. The coordination of the quantity produced at each production point is not automatic but has to be controlled to ensure a balanced flow of parts to the assembly lines.

Batch production can be generally regarded as a compromise between process or mass production, dependent upon the product, and jobbing. The volume is not sufficient to justify the large investment in plant required for process or mass production but is generally greater than that provided by jobbing production. Batch production makes use of common production facilities for producing a variety of products or different sizes or grades of the same product. It can be applied to homogeneous or assembly products. Batch production involves change-over, queuing, control of quantities produced at the different operations and the provision of stores for accumulating and marshalling parts prior to assembly.

Jobbing production operates when an article is made in small quantities to the specification of the customer. The manufacture of special castings is one example. The jobbing manufacturer is generally equipped to produce small quantity items economically through using general-purpose machines that involve the minimum set-up time.

7.2   The production system

Every company has to develop the system that will best suit its product and the economics of its situation. One thing is certain — the appropriate system never emerges without concentrated thinking and effort.

The continuous manufacture of products through process or mass production methods represents the most advanced development. The methods of production are built into the facilities.

Batch manufacture, particularly in its application to the

assembly type of product, has to operate in very different conditions and stores have generally to be provided as a grouping or marshalling point for the accumulation of parts prior to assembly. But some companies have been slow to appreciate that while they cannot apply the principle of continuous production to the product as a whole they may be able to apply it to the manufacture of certain parts.

A large cross-section of industry is engaged in batch production in one form or another. Some of the products are comparatively simple and present no particular production problem. Others can be quite complex and the assembly type of product consisting of a large number of parts is probably the most complicated of all forms of production. It is in this field that opportunities can exist for the partial or limited application of more advanced production methods.

The task is how to condition the manufacturing process to be able to apply, in part at least, the concepts and practices common to continuous production. Manufacture should proceed against a production programme based on sales requirements. The marketing division will provide the information required for preparing the programme; in the case of stocking lines the sales requirement will be based on an assessment; in non-stocking lines it will be based on an analysis of the order book. A surprising number of companies place the onus on the production division to prepare the production programme without any guidance or committment by the marketing division. This is not an uncommon malfunction. The production division is not in the best position to anticipate sales requirements for it has neither the up-to-date knowledge of the markets nor the contacts that are available to the marketing division.

The production planning department operates through the programme supplied by the marketing division. It has to examine the programme from three aspects; (a) the availability of materials and other purchase items; (b) the manufacturing orders that have to be placed on the factory; (c) the work load represented by the programme in relation to production capacity.

The availability of materials will depend on the procurement policy. In the continuous production of standard products it is usual to estimate the requirements for materials and purchased components for a period and to place contract orders accordingly with deliveries to be made against delivery schedules. Deliveries may be arranged on a daily or a weekly basis or other short term period.

In batch manufacture annual or period contracts may be placed for certain raw materials that are used in quantity. Wherever practical it is better to place orders for quantities and to arrange for deliveries against schedule. But economics enter into this.

The procedure frequently applied in batch production due to the restriction in volume is to fix a minimum stock level and reorder quantity for each item and to place a replenishment order when the minimum stock level is reached. This is a straightforward system to operate and is suitable for relatively inexpensive items but it requires careful control in its application to expensive items to avoid an excessive inventory.

It is probably exceptional in batch manufacture of assembly products to have the volume to justify calling materials and parts from suppliers at short intervals in view of the higher prices for small quantities. Many companies have to arrange a two to three months' requirement in one delivery from the supplier to obtain an economic price. The same conditions can apply to manufactured parts where batches equivalent to two to three months' requirement have to be produced at a time to justify the cost involved in setting up machines.

Companies are now making a closer study of the parts contained in a product to see if more expensive items can be singled out for special treatment with regard to shorter delivery periods or shorter production periods as a means of reducing the inventory without increasing costs. This is simply an application of Pareto's law. In a product it generally means that 80 per cent of the value is contributed by 20 per cent of the number of components.

The conditions mentioned largely apply to the batch production of engineering products where many materials are generally involved and many parts together with a multiplicity of machining operations. Outside of engineering, particularly in process production, fewer materials are involved and fewer manufacturing operations. This simplifies procurement and production.

In engineering products some companies have found that a few of the most costly items can be procured against delivery schedules at economic prices. Also that one or two costly items can justify the investment in plant necessary for line production. These parts are fed directly to the assembly line and the quick throughput time and the consequent reduction in the inventory compensates for the increased investment in plant.

7.3   Production organisation

Every company has to develop the organisation that will best suit the products and the volume of production. Production is a practical function and the plan of the organisation must be specifically geared to efficient performance with due regard to the competence and skills required for each activity.

The major activities normally undertaken by a production organisation can be broadly summarised as:

1   *Methods engineering* which decides the methods and the means of manufacture.
2   *Work study* which is concerned with operating performance and the time factor of production.
3   *Production planning* which decides the production programmes and procurement and manufacturing schedules that will maximise output and give the optimum service to customers.
4   *Purchasing.* The procurement of materials and purchased items at the right time, in the right quantity, of the right quality and at economic prices in accordance with the procurement schedules or purchase requisitions placed by production planning department.
5   *Personnel management.* This department performs a wide variety of functions. One of its primary functions is the recruitment of personnel.
6   *Production function.* This refers to the production function proper which produces the goods.

7   *Quality control.* This department ensures that specifications and standards are prescribed where necessary for all purchased items and manufactured parts and products and that adequate inspection is carried out to maintain these standards.
8   *Plant maintenance.* This department is responsible for maintaining the plant in good working condition. Its primary function is to avoid breakdowns and its efficiency is generally measured on this basis. Many maintenance departments have developed preventative maintenance procedures to ensure the minimum disruption of production through breakdowns.

Most of these departments and functions are common to every industrial enterprise although titles may vary.

Some of the functions mentioned are described in more detail below.

7.3.1   Methods engineering

This function deals with the technical aspects of production. It plans the methods of production, it provides the production facilities and designs jigs, tools and fixtures.

The methods of production may be built-in when designing the plant as is generally the practice in continuous production. In batch production where common facilities have to be used in the production of the products the methods have to be more flexible.

Batch production has to be concerned not only with the methods but with the economics of the situation. It is not a question of deciding the best methods of production and the facilities appropriate to them but the best method in the circumstances. This is a question of matching methods with volume.

Volume is an important factor and a company cannot be competitive if it has to sacrifice efficiency for economy, unless its competitors are in the same position.

7.3.2 Work study

Methods engineering and work study are closely interrelated and both functions are normally controlled by the methods engineer. Work study is not technical in the sense of methods engineering although there are many techniques associated with it. Work study is generally concerned with the efficiency attained in implementing the methods prescribed by the methods engineering function. Its function is operational and it tends to centre on the operator and the operations with a view to reducing effort and time. It provides quantitative standards for measuring performance and output. But its duties can be widely extended to almost any job that requires trained and skilled observations.

7.3.3 Production planning and control

This function is concerned with obtaining the output required in terms of quantity and time. The technical function, or methods engineering, has decided 'how' the products will be produced and has provided the production facilities. The work study function has defined the production times. This combined information enables the planning function to programme production in accordance with the sales programme submitted by the marketing division with due regard to the total production capacity of the plant.

Production planning in continuous production is generally a standardised and well established procedure and does not present many difficulties other than procuring the materials required in the right quantity and at the right time. The planning and control of batch manufacture, particularly in engineering products, can be more involved due to the necessity of changing machines and queuing.

7.3.4 Production activity

This is the hub of the business, the operating centre that converts plans and instructions into output. This is the point of reality where performance is compared with the planned expectation and where any causes of failure are identified — and these can be many and varied. The production function proper can generally be divided into:

1   The factors that are directly related to production itself.
2   The auxiliary functions that aid production but are not part of it.
3   The service functions and administration.

In many factories the productive operators are outnumbered by those employed in the supporting activities and with increasing mechanisation and automation the gap is widening. Productivity is increasingly a factor of man and machine but in view of the large capital investment involved the importance of the operator and his performance is not diminished but increasing.

The direct factors of production can be summarised as the productive operators, the machine setters, the machines and their maintenance. It follows that the direct costs of production are the wages of the productive operators and the machine setters, the cost of machines as represented by depreciation and maintenance, the cost of tools, power costs, miscellaneous supplies and the charge for floor space. These are important considerations in evaluating productivity and the costs of production.

The auxiliary activities are concerned with the movements of materials to and from the machines, general labouring and supervision. The supporting services and administration usually include storekeeping, inspection, methods engineering and work study, production planning and control, purchasing, the personnel function and factory management.

Figure 7.1 shows an organisation chart for a typical engineering factory, but it has to be appreciated that organisations can vary considerably.

7.4   Measuring performance and productivity

In essence production performance is measured by comparing the output achieved against the production programme. But it does not always follow that performance can be accepted as a

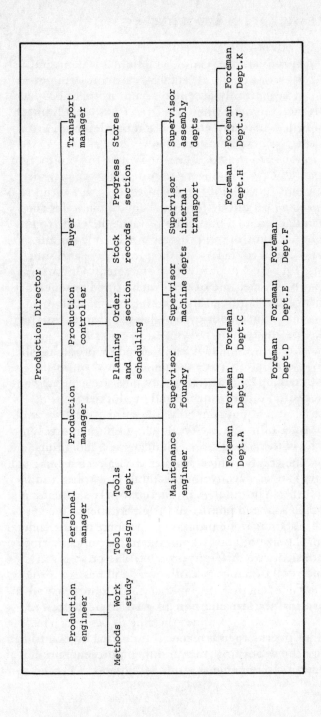

Figure 7.1 Production organisation chart

measure of productivity.

Where the production cycle of the product is comparatively short and the work in progress is fairly constant then performance can be generally accepted as a measure of productivity. This measurement where applicable has the advantages of being direct, simple and effective and the degree of 'error that can arise is generally insignificant.

In continuous process manufacture (where the production cycle is generally short and work-in-progress constant) the output can almost invariably be regarded as both a measure of performance and productivity. In a chemical plant designed for the manufacture of a particular product the cycle time was three hours and work-in-progress was fairly constant. Output was compared daily with the programme and summarised in a four-weekly production statement. Output was accepted both as a measure of performance and productivity as the variance was confined to a fluctuation in work-in-progress within a three-hour cycle — insignificant against a four-weekly production period.

In the continuous manufacture of assembly products where there is flow production, for example, motor cars, the quantities emerging from the assembly lines are generally an accurate measure of performance and productivity.

In batch production it generally follows that performance is not a measure of productivity. Batch production involves change-overs with varying sizes of batches and short runs which must inevitably reduce productivity. Nevertheless productivity can be effectively and simple controlled in this type of industry. The batch manufacture of glass paper and emery cloth is a case in point. All the glass paper and emery cloth go through the same process on the same plant. Each variation in the size of grain deposited on the paper or cloth virtually constitutes a different product. The process starts with a jumbo roll of paper or cloth every roll being approximately the same length. The paper or cloth to be selected is dependent upon the size and type of grain to be deposited. The size of grain also determines the glue to be used. The jumbo roll of paper or cloth receives its coating of glue to be followed by the deposit of grain and then proceeds through a drying operation to emerge as a finished jumbo roll ready to be cut into appropriate size sheets. Once the plant has been set-up for a batch the whole process is continuous and fully mechanised. An average productivity standard has been developed to show the average number of jumbo rolls that should be processed in the production period.

The number of jumbo rolls of the same type contained in a batch can vary according to the sales demand for each type. This means that the total number of jumbo rolls produced in the production period, which decides productivity, can also vary.

Two controls are in operation: (a) the number of jumbo rolls produced in relation to the production programme, and (b) the total number of jumbo rolls produced as compared with the standard set and if this shows an unsatisfactory deviation a detailed investigation follows.

The manufacture of assembly products in batches can pose a wide variety of conditions. In many products performance is a fair indication of productivity, for example, in the clothing trade where assembly closely follows cutting. But there are many companies that cannot measure productivity in natural units of output and have to resort to synthetic measurements, usually the standard hour as defined by work study. This is particularly true of the batch manufacture of assembly products in the engineering industry and a large number of companies are in this category.

The measurement of productivity through the application of synthetics will be considered in detail in production budgeting.

7.5 Summary

No two manufacturing concerns are alike and the production organisation and methods must be geared to the particular circumstances of the business. The limitations imposed by the products and the volume of production have to be recognised but within these limits the opportunity should be taken to exploit every possibility.

Wherever practicable production should be properly programmed and output should be compared with the programme to measure performance. This is an important measure in production planning and control. It does not always follow that performance is a measure of productivity and alternative means have to be established for controlling it.

8 Production Planning and Inventory Control

Inventory control of production materials is a function of production planning which is designed to ensure that materials are available for production in the required quantity at the required time and with the minimum feasible investment.

Production planning is concerned with quantities in all their varied forms; quantities of the various raw materials in stock, quantities of finished parts made or purchased in stock, work-in-progress in all its aspects — in short overall stock control. It thinks in terms of items and quantities in stock and only indirectly in financial values.

An inventory represents the investment in stocks at a particular time and inventory control can only be realised through effective stock control — a factor that is not always fully appreciated.

To maintain inventories at an absolute minimum level would not be practical or economical as it would periodically give rise to shortages of materials for production. An important factor in stock control and, therefore, inventory control is to decide reasonable safety margins.

The type of product and the volume of its production can influence the degree of control that can be exercised in maintaining inventories at a low level. A greater degree of control can be expected from continuous production than is generally possible in intermittent production.

Control of the stock of finished products is generally the responsibility of the marketing division rather than a function of production control.

8.1   Analysis of the product: materials

The materials content of the product has to be defined. In the assembly type of product for example it will be necessary to know:

1   The parts that are contained in the product, the number of each per finished unit and if these have to be manufactured or purchased.
2   The material and the quantity required to make each part.
3   A list of the sub-assemblies that go into final assembly and a parts list for each sub-assembly.

In process manufacture the different raw materials used to make the product and the quantity of each material will be listed. The yield expected is also another important factor in many process industries.

8.2   Analysis of the product: operations

Operation study is a technical process that demands technical training and experience of the particular products and processes.

Reverting to the assembly type of engineering product the information generally required can be summed up as:

1   The best method of making the particular part.
2   The operations that have to be performed in making each part and the machines and tools to be used.
3   The sequence of operations.
4   The time required to perform each operation subdivided between set-up time and producing time.
5   The economic batch size for the production of each part.
6   Determining the sub-division of assembly work as between sub-assemblies and final assembly; stating the time required for each sub-assembly and for final assembly.

In the process manufacture of a single, or homogeneous, product the total processing time is required. In batch processing the set-up time and the total production time for the product are required.

8.3   Production programmes

The programming of production can be influenced by the
product and the production volume. The product may be
standard or it may be standard with minor modifications to
suit the customer or it may be made to customer specification as in jobbing work. There is the further distinction that
standard products may be stocked or produced against actual
orders received. There is a wide diversification in conditions
and circumstances.

The most advanced application of production methods is
to be found in continuous manufacture; the processing of a
single, or homogeneous, product in a plant exclusively designed for the purpose or the mass production of assembly
products where machines are permanently set up to do all or
most of the production operations.

These are the obvious methods to be used for manufacturing
products but they can only be applied economically where the
volume is sufficient to support the comparatively large investment in plant.

For most products intermittent production is the only
feasible method. This is a case of using common production
facilities to manufacture different products or several sizes of
the same product. It is not a question of deciding the best
method and the best production facilities but the best compromise that will suit the economics of the situation. These
circumstances can influence the method of programming
production which is generally simpler and more effective in
continuous manufacture.

Where it is necessary for production to anticipate sales (as
in the case of stocking lines), the best practice suggests that
the marketing division should state the requirements to
enable a production programme to be prepared. The production planning department will check the requirements
against the capacity of the plant to ensure that it is capable of
achievement. It will then go forward for top management
approval. The same principle frequently applies to the stocking
of standard parts where the finished products can only be
completed against orders received.

Where manufacture can only proceed against orders received

it is quite usual for the production planning department to prepare the production programme. Alternatively the marketing division may analyse the orders and submit requirements to production control for programming.

What the stocking lines should be can be a vexed question. Obviously the marketing division will always press for products to be stocked to give a selling advantage. But it is not always prepared to commit itself by submitting a statement of requirements to be incorporated in a production programme.

It is important that production programmes should be prepared far enough ahead to provide the lead time necessary to procure materials and parts that are not carried in stock, or to supply delivery schedules to suppliers in respect of bulk orders placed. The duration of the programme should be carefully decided with due regard to the production cycle time of the product(s).

8.4   Production scheduling

Once the programme is completed and approved, schedules are prepared by the production planning department detailing materials to be procured and production requirements and the time limits to be observed.

The starting date of the programme should be the date when production is due to commence. Where materials or parts have to be specially purchased the programme should be issued far enough in advance to provide the lead time for procurement. Likewise, if it is the practice to place bulk orders for call-off against delivery schedules, time must be allowed to give suppliers due notice.

In some industries it is not necessary to compile production programmes at regular intervals. The practice is to issue a production programme which remains in operation until an amended programme is issued. In like manner the production schedule remains unchanged until the programme changes. Companies that operate in this manner generally review the sales position and sales prospects at regular intervals and decide if a change in the production programme is warranted.

Industries that can operate the same production programme over an extended period are generally engaged in continuous manufacture.

It has to be impressed upon the organisation that programmes and schedules are made to be achieved. Where programmes are regularly achieved it indicates that the labour force and the production facilities are being employed effectively, that delivery services to customers are under control and that the inventory is not excessive through unbalanced production.

8.5 Procurement

The procurement of materials is the first stage in the manufacturing process. Ideally the objective is to receive materials as and when the production process demands them. The nearest approach to this is to place bulk orders for short term deliveries against a delivery schedule. The quantities to be called for on delivery schedules must be adequate to provide the supplier with an economic production run or the purchase price will be substantially increased if the order is accepted.

Not every company (probably only a very small number) is in a position to satisfy these conditions and the economics of the situation demand an alternative procedure. From the inventory viewpoint stocks are at their lowest when short-term deliveries can be arranged.

The alternative is to ascertain the minimum delivery quantities that will warrant economic purchase prices and to place orders accordingly. This may be operated through a minimum stock and re-order quantity procedure. The information required to operate this procedure is the average weekly or monthly rate of usage and the lead time required that is the time that will elapse from raising the purchase requisition to receiving the goods. The usage per week, or month, multiplied by the lead time gives the minimum stock quantity. It is usual to increase this to provide a safety margin.

If the weekly rate of usage is 1000, the lead time six weeks and the safety margin two weeks then the minimum stock will be fixed at 8000 (8 × 1000). The re-order quantity

cannot be fixed at less than six weeks but there are a number
of factors that may warrant an increase in the quantity. It may
be necessary to order a larger quantity to obtain an economic
purchase price or to reduce the cost of raising purchase
orders. In either event the average quantity held in stock will
be increased and this will increase the inventory.

The procedure of re-ordering when the minimum stock
level is reached is simple to operate and can be applied very
effectively to low-priced items. But expensive items should be
under more direct control wherever feasible. Here the objective should be to place orders for deferred deliveries at
economic prices and to arrange suitable delivery periods
with the suppliers.

8.6   Production

The principles to be observed in procurement largely apply to
production. The aim should be to apply the flow-line principle
wherever practicable as in continuous production. This
shortens the production cycle time, keeps work-in-progress to
a minimum and maintains the inventory at the lowest level.
Where the production volume does not justify the large investment in plant frequently required for continuous production
then a company should examine the possibilities for its
partial application to particular sections of production.

The difficulties encountered in intermittent production
can vary with the industry. Processing in batches involves
change-over time but in all other respects the process may be
continuous. Many assembly industries are engaged in the
manufacture of simple products. The batch manufacture of
assembly type engineering products can be very involved
comprising many parts and a large number of operations.
Change-over time can represent a fairly high proportion of the
total production time and for this reason the aim must be to
produce economic batches where the quantity to be made
justifies the time required to set up machines. The economic
batch is generally determined by the relation of operating
time to setting up time. Some companies operate on nothing
less than a four-to-one or five-to-one ratio which means that

the operational time is four or five times greater than the set-up time. The production cycle time for the component is further extended by unavoidable queuing between operations.

8.7   Production planning

The organisation and procedures associated with production planning can vary considerably between companies.

The type of product and the volume of production have a marked influence. In continuous manufacture it generally follows that procurement and production can be more effectively organised and controlled than is possible in batch manufacture. This applies in particular to the manufacture of engineering products.

In stressing certain important aspects, management can also influence the planning procedure. And there is always the over-riding consideration — is the planning system adequate to meet the particular requirements of the business?

An example follows of the application of a planning procedure by a company manufacturing engineering products. The example has been chosen because it relates to batch production and illustrates many of the principles involved in production planning and control. It is not put forward as an outstanding application but as an illustration of the thinking that has gone into developing a system that copes reasonably well with the particular conditions — conditions that are more or less common to a large number of companies.

8.7.1   The products

The company manufactures electrical equipment, some of which is standard and some made to the particular requirements of the customer. The standard products have many deviations and production is governed by the orders received except in a few isolated instances. The equipment manufactured to customer requirements is likewise dependent upon orders received.

A large proportion of the orders received for standard and

made-to-order equipment represents bulk requirements with deferred deliveries usually on a monthly basis. Because of the average size of the order book the company has a lead time of three to four months for standard equipment and at least six months for made-to-order equipment.

8.7.2   The production process

There are four assembly lines subdivided into small, medium and large equipment and another line for assembling the principal range of standard equipment. All assembly lines with the exception of the standard equipment line, handle made-to-order equipment and sundry standard equipment. There is a sub-assembly section that produces all the sub-assemblies required by the four assembly lines.

There are four feeder departments. The metal fabrication department produces the sheet metal cases that house the equipment and also other sundry requirements. There are two sections to this department: the metal working section that produces the parts and the welding section that assembles them into cases. There is also the paint shop that paints the cases, a machine shop that produces a various assortment of parts and the transformer department which produces transformers and sundry electrical items.

The objective is to feed the manufactured items direct to the assembly lines wherever practicable. Manufacture for stock is only arranged where this is essential for producing in economic batch quantities. In the metal fabrication department, for example, storage facilities are provided for the parts comprised in a case to justify economic production runs. Parts have to be made and stored in sets. These parts are only welded into cases to meet the assembly requirements.

All parts made by the machine shop are produced in batches and stored in the finished parts store on a max-min basis.

Transformers are made as required for assembly. Electrical parts are treated in the same manner as machined parts.

The components that are fed directly to assembly — cases, transformers and sub-assemblies — may be ready on schedule but assembly may not be quite ready to receive them. A limited space is provided in these departments to store the components until assembly can use them.

Particular importance is attached to two factors: the synchronisation of feeder departments and assembly lines and the production of parts in economic batch quantities. The company does not as a general practice encourage excessive production runs since experience has shown that these are usually achieved at the expense of other items that are required.

8.7.3 Production programming

Planning is centred on the assembly lines. Information is regularly maintained to show the work load ahead of each assembly line as represented by outstanding orders. Programmes are prepared on a monthly basis and if an assembly line has a six months work load this would be represented by six monthly programmes.

As orders are received they are added to the work load. The assembly hours required for a particular order are obtained from the quotation file where the product is nonstandard or from the standards file where it is a standard product. The production planning department knows from its records the average number of production hours that can be obtained daily from each assembly line. This figure multiplied by the number of days in the month measures the capacity of the respective assembly lines. When the orders loaded into the month through the orders received reach this capacity figure the monthly programme is closed.

The assembly lines are not inflexible. If one assembly line is loaded far ahead of another then an attempt is made to balance the loads but the scope for interchangeability is limited.

The assembly programmes arranged in the manner stated provide the basis for:

1   Quoting reliable delivery dates against enquiries received.
2   Procuring items that are particular to an order or which are not carried in stock.

3   Preparing production programmes for the feeder departments.

8.7.4   Procurement

Policies associated with the procurement of materials have
evolved through experience over a long period. Since the
conditions commit the company to the batch manufacture
of products which cannot generally be made for stock the
system aims at achieving the best compromise to meet the
situation.

The major raw materials — steel sheet, angle, bar and copper
wire — are ordered in bulk for monthly delivery. Other raw
materials are on a max-min basis. In the case of copper wire
the bulk order does not specify sizes. The particular sizes
required are notified one month in advance of delivery.

Purchased components constitute a substantial proportion
of total purchases. Components that are used regularly are
controlled on a max-min basis. In this connection the company made a careful study of the components stocked and
the rationalisation that followed considerably reduced the
varieties needed in stock.

In manufacturing equipment to order it invariably follows
that certain components have to be ordered specially. Since it
is the general policy for customers to place bulk orders for
deferred delivery the company pursues the same policy in
dealing with its suppliers. Orders for special components are
placed four months ahead of assembly but this can be extended or shortened according to the delivery situation.
Every purchase order clearly states the date delivery is required, usually the first week of a month, and suppliers are
advised not to shorten or extend this date.

8.7.5   Feeder department programmes

Two programmes are issued to the metal-fabrication departments, one for producing the parts for cases required by
assembly in two months and the other for the assembly

(welding) of cases required by assembly in the following month.

Where the quantity of parts shown on the programme for any job does not constitute an economic production batch then the batch quantity is increased and the surplus placed in stores; this presumes that it is a continuing job. Conversely if there are sufficient sets of parts in stores for a job on the programme then a production order is not issued.

Two programmes are issued to the transformer department, one showing the assembly requirements two months ahead and the other one month ahead. Transformers vary in size and in the cycle time required to produce them. Those that require more than one month to produce are shown on the two-monthly programme. These same transformers will appear the following month in the monthly programme.

A programme is issued to the sub-assembly department showing the sub-assemblies required by the assembly department in the following month. The programme is arranged to show the assembly department requirements in weeks.

No programmes are issued for the manufacture of small electrical parts and machined parts which are produced on a max-min basis and delivered to the finished parts stores on completion.

All programmes are carefully checked to ensure that the capacity is available to meet the programme. Capacity is measured in the manner indicated for the assembly lines. The number of production hours obtainable per day is multiplied by the number of days in the month to arrive at the capacity in hours. The time required for each job on the programme is known and the total hours included in the programme must not exceed the capacity hours. Where there are special-purpose machines, as in the metal-fabrication department, care is taken not to overload these machines.

A production order is issued in card form for every job appearing on the programme together with the appropriate drawings and job cards. Orders are issued in the same form for other jobs that are not programmed, for example, the manufacture of electrical and machined parts. As jobs are completed the order card is returned to the production planning department and these are marked off on the programmes.

This is the method of progressing programmed jobs.

In the case of orders for electrical and machined parts these are recorded in the order section of the appropriate stock cards and signals are placed on the visible edges of the cards. When an order card is returned on completion of the job the quantity produced is added to the stock quantity on the stock card and the signal removed. Signals which appear on cards after the due date for completion indicate the orders to be chased.

The considerations so far have been concerned with the regulated flow of manufactured parts to the assembly lines to meet the assembly programmes. Another consideration is to ensure that purchased components are available to meet the assembly programmes.

As purchased components are ordered the orders are recorded on the stock cards. When acknowledgements of orders have been received confirming or amending the delivery dates these are recorded on the stock cards and signals are placed on the visible edges of the cards. The stock cards are scrutinised regularly and if a delivery date is exceeded the supplier is contacted immediately. If this results in an amended delivery exceeding a few days this is recorded on the stock card and the signal altered. Amended delivery dates are recorded on a daily report as a means of adjusting the assembly programme if necessary.

A monthly assembly programme for all assembly lines is issued about two weeks prior to the start of the month.

The final stage prior to assembly is the marshalling or kitting of components. Assembly parts lists are issued to the finished parts stores for every order appearing on the assembly programme. It is a rule that an assembly parts list must not be issued to the stores if there is any part that is not available in stock.

As the assembly programmes are arranged by weeks, marshalling starts with the requirements for the first week. The parts are selected for each order and transferred to an assembly stores adjacent to the finished parts stores which is under the control of the assembly foreman. As parts are transferred to the assembly stores the matching components — cases, transformers and sub-assemblies — are collected from the respec-

tive departments and located in the assembly area. The parts
are withdrawn from the assembly stores as required.

Any orders on the assembly programme that are not completed in the month are included in the programme for the
following month. These are usually shown separately on an
overdue list. The work load represented by the overdue items
is shown and also the weeks in which they should be assembled.

The company will not allow overdue orders to accumulate.
The calculation of the work load for the assembly department
is based on normal working hours and overdue orders are held
in check through overtime working.

A major control is the output achieved against the assembly
programme. The production director in his monthly board
report has to comment on performance and explain any fail-
ures to meet the programme. Figures have to be submitted
based on sales values. The orders on the monthly assembly
programme are translated into sales values and the same procedure is adopted for the output achieved; the difference is
the measure of performance. A figure has to be shown for all
overdue orders based on sales values.

8.7.6   The production planning organisation

Before the present production planning system was developed
the emphasis was on limiting the staff from the viewpoint
that it was a non-productive operation. The shortcomings of
the planning procedure — overdue deliveries, excessive work
in progress, extended production cycles and a large inventory
— forced the company to recognise the importance of the
planning function. The first step was to decide what the
company required and then to create the organisation to
achieve it. The objective was not to save staff but to save the
time of executives in dealing with customer complaints and
to make the planning procedure effective. The production
planning manager heads the department. In addition to super-
vising the general operations of the department he is closely
involved in preparing and controlling the assembly programmes. The programming of the feeder departments is
largely delegated to the leader of the programming and

progress section.

The production planning department comprises the following main sections:

1   *Planning and progress section.* This section has the dual function of preparing production programmes and ensuring their implementation. In addition to preparing the programmes it has to submit schedules to the purchasing department for procuring components from suppliers that are special to orders or not carried in stock. It also projects the usage of steel and copper for the purchases department. It has to control the progress of orders against the programmes of the feeder departments and to see that purchased components are available as required by the assembly lines. It is responsible for issuing assembly parts lists to the stores for marshalling after verifying that all the components for an order are available. The programming and progressing is departmentalised and departments are allocated to persons. Responsibility is clearly defined.

2   *Stock control section.* This section keeps stock cards for purchased components, manufactured electrical and machined parts and fabricated parts. The stock cards show the orders placed and the quantities received or produced, issues and the balance in stock. Signals on the edges of the cards are used for progressing orders.

3   *Production order section.* This section issues production orders in card form together with the appropriate job cards and drawings. The return of the order cards on completion of jobs enables the programming and progress section to keep track of the progress.

8.7.7   *General remarks*

The company is fortunate in that the order book provides the lead time necessary for the procurement of materials and parts generally and for special parts particularly and the production programme can, therefore, be based entirely on the production capacity. The work load and not the dates special parts will be received decides the delivery dates to customers.

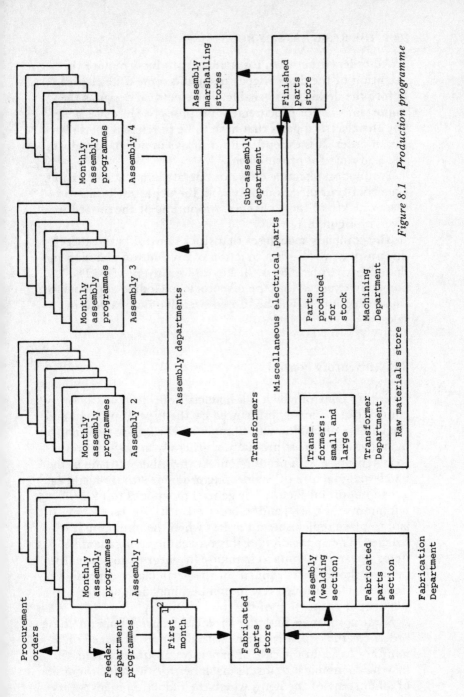

Figure 8.1 Production programme

All orders other than for standard products require the attention of the design department and some time elapses before the details are available. The electrical design is the important one for procurement purposes because it is generally the electrical parts that have to be purchased specially for an order. It is exceptional for delays in design to reduce the lead time for procurement.

Production planning does not operate in a static situation. Changes occur in various ways and the department has to react quickly to these changes. An outline of the procedure is given in Figure 8.1.

The company recognises that stock control — and therefore inventory control — is a function of production planning and that effective planning is the key to low inventories. The company expects that the inventory, excluding any stock of finished products, will be turned over five times a year in sales.

8.8   Inventory control

Inventory control which is a financial reflection of stock control can be largely influenced by the type of product and the volume of production. Companies engaged in continuous manufacture or mass production generally arrange deliveries to synchronise with production. At the other extreme in the batch manufacture of engineering products storage facilities are an important factor. The general practice is to fix a minimum stock level and re-order quantity for each item and to place replenishment orders when the minimum level is reached. The application of this procedure to inexpensive items is warranted but to minimise inventories an alternative method should be examined for the particularly expensive items which, although few in number, may account for a substantial proportion of the total inventory.

Some companies find it economical to place bulk purchase orders for the expensive items with deliveries arranged on a monthly basis. In the case of expensive production items it may be economical to install machines for the line-production of all or some of the items where the reduction in inventory and a shorter manufacturing cycle may well compensate for the larger investment in plant.

These are guidelines for inventory control but it is important to recognise that stock control which determines the value of the investment is an integral part of the planning function. It follows that effective inventory control is dependent upon effective production planning; the objective should be to ensure that materials and parts are available to production in the right quantity, in the right quality and at the right time. Additional stocks as a safety margin should be maintained at a justifiable level.

The essence of inventory control is movement and a regulated flow of materials. The constant aim should be to reduce the production cycle time of the products and to increase the rate of inventory turnover to sales. This has the effect of reducing the congestion of materials in the pipeline. In many companies work-in-progress represents a high proportion of the inventory and not infrequently there is scope for reducing it. Congestion of materials in the pipeline is measured not only by the cost of the materials but also by the labour and overheads incurred.

Top management has to exercise judgement on inventories through overall ratios. The ratio most commonly used is the number of times the inventory is turned over through sales in the course of a year (the annual sales figure divided by the average value of the inventory).

Reverting to the batch manufacture of engineering products, the inventory generally comprises raw materials in stock, finished parts in stock and work-in-progress. Where a company can subdivide its inventory into these three sections then it can obtain a closer control but it has to be noted that the work entailed in making this analysis can be considerable and probably not always worth the effort unless there is a computer application.

Where feasible, each of these inventories can be related to the average monthly cost of the parts used on the assembly lines and ratios established for control purposes. The cost of parts used on assembly will comprise material and factory labour and overheads cost, or purchase price if bought out.

8.9 Summary

Production planning has to be geared to the end product and to the quantity required to meet the production programme which in the case of standard products for stock will be based on information provided by the marketing division and for non-standard products on the sales order book.

Production planning in continuous manufacture does not generally present any major problems. The same is largely true in batch processing and batch assembly work of a large variety of products. In the batch manufacture of engineering assembly products production planning can be an involved procedure. The production and purchase of parts have to be related to the requirements of the assembly programme and priorities fixed accordingly. It normally follows that there cannot be a direct flow of all parts from the feeder departments to assembly and stores have to be provided as a location and marshalling point.

At all stages of production it is essential to ensure that the work load imposed by the programme is properly related to the production capacity and with due regard to economic production runs. In the purchase or batch manufacture of parts it can sometimes be worth making a distinction between the major and the minor parts in the procedure adopted.

A comparison of the programmed assembly output with the actual output achieved should be recognised as an essential control over performance. The same applies, of course, to process manufacture.

Production planning and control is an area that is never free from problems; in periods of industrial prosperity the procurement of certain materials in short supply becomes difficult and unreliable and in periods of depression the sales order book shrinks. There are also the problems that are created inside the business. A company must ensure that its production planning system is adaptable to change and free from self-inflicted problems such as quoting delivery dates to customers that are not founded on well established work loads.

Good inventory control is a corollary of effective production planning.

9 The Production Budget

The annual sales budget and the inventory requirements provide the framework for the production budget.

Certain problems may be inherent in the production function dependent upon the nature of the products, the degree of product standardisation, the volume of production and the financial resources of the company. The procurement of production materials is a case in point. Generally the most effective method of procuring materials is to place bulk orders on suppliers, probably on an annual basis, with frequent deliveries against an agreed schedule. This tends to reduce purchase prices and to reduce inventories. But the volume of business must be sufficient to make short-term deliveries practicable at an economic price and management must be reasonably confident in the quality of the products and the consistency of sales demand. Where a company makes non-standard products it will be limited in its procurement procedure. Where a company cannot justify the placing of bulk orders for periodical call-off it is usual to fix minimum stock levels and a re-order quantity for materials that are regularly used. When the minimum stock level is reached an order is placed for the re-order quantity specified. Purchase prices are generally higher under this arrangement and inventories cannot easily be maintained at a minimal level.

Another factor of importance is how far the company is prepared to increase the inventory of finished products to maintain production at a constant level during a period of fluctuating sales. These are two of the more important factors that require a statement of company policy.

A production budget does not mean the same thing to all companies. One of its primary and generally accepted purposes is to determine the production costs for the volume of output required. The production costs are translated into product costs and into cost of sales to enable the profit budget to be prepared.

Management practices vary in how far the business should be committed to the production budget beyond projecting product costs for a profit budget. In general most companies, at least the progressive ones, will accept the technical R&D and product design cost budget and that of the marketing division as they know that the future prospects of the business will be largely conditioned by these functions. The cost budget for administration is generally acceptable. It is with the production budget that differences generally arise.

An engineering company has been operating an annual budget in conjunction with long-term strategic planning for many years. Its products have always been good, some the leaders in their particular fields, and the company has shown a steady expansion. The marketing organisation is efficient.

Through the experience gained over the years the budget scheme has been progressively improved and it can be reasonably stated that the company has acquired the art of budgeting in its main essentials.

In the early stages of the scheme an annual sales budget was accepted if it showed an improvement on the previous year and provided a balanced work load that largely utilised the production capacity. Later it was decided that the annual sales budget should be subdivided into quarterly periods. One year the marketing division demonstrated that the sales order intake matched the budget and that the production division was therefore responsible for the failure to produce the budgeted output. The production division was able to prove that the order intake was not consistent with production requirements and that a large proportion of the orders had been received in the last three months of the year.

The company decided to subdivide the sales budget into quarterly periods for the following reasons:

1   The subdivision into quarters would enable the production division to take the fluctuations in the order intake if any into account in budgeting the production output.

2   The quarterly budgets would not be a subdivision of the annual budget on an arbitrary basis. The analysis had to be factual and justifiable.

3   The company would have the option of increasing the inventories over a short period to stabilise production.

As a further development it was decided that the marketing division would place a quarterly programme on the production division for each product line. In this connection it should be mentioned that production was organised by product divisions and in practice a programme was issued for each division. The programmes had to be issued in advance to give the production planning department the lead time required to adjust the delivery schedules for materials with suppliers. It was the standard practice for a meeting to be held between the marketing division and the production division to discuss the quarterly programmes and their implications from the manufacturing viewpoint. The emphasis was generally on the utilisation of labour and production capacity. In general the normal fluctuations in the programme presented no particular problems. But it was generally understood that if a programme could not productively employ the labour force or was beyond the capacity of the number employed that a meeting should be arranged with the managing director to hammer out decisions such as making for stock or reducing overtime working or at the other extreme employing more labour.

The policy of the company was clear on the procedure for quarterly programming. The marketing division had to project the programmes on a factual appraisal of the current and short-term situation without regard to the budget. Once the programmes were agreed on the lines indicated above it was the policy of the company to implement them. The marketing division was responsible for the validity of the programmes and for the inventory of finished products. The production division in conjunction with the cost department projected the costs against the programmes and performance was measured by comparing the output obtained and the costs incurred.

It was the practice to place annual contracts on suppliers and for deliveries to be arranged against delivery schedules.

This example has been discussed at length because it shows how an efficient and progressive company operates in a situation that must be common to very many companies. Although the company operates through quarterly production budgets all financial statements and reports compare the performance for the month and the year to date against the annual budget.

9.1   Budget information

A production budget will generally show the products to be produced during the year and the quantity of each. It is preferable to subdivide the annual budget into shorter periods to measure the consistency of the order intake in relation to production requirements. This will give management the opportunity to formulate a policy on making for stock in the short term to stabilise production and costs. The budget must project the labour requirements. It is usual to express this by departments showing the number to be employed in the different grades. This information provides the basis for preparing a payroll budget.

The costs involved in operating the production division should be arranged in accordance with responsibilities. The grouping may be done by departments or by functions and sub-functions but whatever basis is adopted responsibility for the costs incurred must be clearly defined. In the same manner standards should be established for measuring performance.

The head of a department or supervisor may be responsible for the number of persons employed in the department but not generally for the wages and salaries incurred as rates of pay are usually outside his jurisdiction. In many companies a number of persons are assigned to each department and the 'headcount' cannot be increased without the authority of a high ranking official.

The products to be produced during the year as detailed by the budget will provide the basis for determining the materials requirement and this will be translated into a purchases budget if it is the practice of the company to place bulk orders for supplies.

A production budget has to provide all the information required to project the costs of production and to translate them into product costs and cost of sales. The budgets normally comprised in a production budget are:

1   *An output budget.* This projects the products and the quantity of each to be made.
2   *Purchases budget.* The products and the quantity of each to be made provides the basis for developing a purchases budget.
3   *Payroll budget.* The labour requirements, i.e. the total number of persons to be employed and in what capacity, permit a payroll budget to be prepared.
4   *Expenses budget.* This has to be an assessment of the various expenses that will be incurred and the amount. The level of production capacity projected by the budget will provide the guidelines for this assessment.
5   *Materials cost budget.* The basic information used in developing the purchases budget will provide a basis for the materials cost budget as mentioned later.

The payroll budget, the expenses budget and the materials cost budget will conjointly give the total cost of production.

Some production budgets make reference to plant requirements but these are generally long-term arrangements as very little can be achieved within the short span of an annual budget.

9.2   The production cost structure

The production costs can be broadly subdivided into the materials cost and the cost of operating the production division.

The factor necessary for projecting production costs is the quantity to be produced of each product. The materials cost is established by identifying the materials used in the product and the quantity of each, applying the purchase price, or standard price, of each material and summarising the results to arrive at the total cost. The total materials cost for each product is multiplied by the quantity to be produced to arrive at the total materials cost for the budgeted output of that product. This procedure is repeated for each product. The aggregate material costs for all products is the total required for the budget.

It is important to recognise the structure of production operating costs. These should be subdivided into:

The factors that are directly related to production itself.
The auxiliary factors that aid production but are not part of it.
The service functions.
Administration functions.

These can be developed in greater detail as follows:

1   *Direct operating costs*
    a   Plant operating costs. These will include depreciation, plant maintenance, and power.
    b   Direct labour costs. The wages paid to all operators directly involved in production, for example, machine operators and setters.
    c   Establishment charges, or space cost. These comprise heating, lighting, rent, rates, insurance, maintenance of buildings and depreciation.

2   *Indirect production costs.* These relate to the indirect costs incurred by the production departments, which will include the movement of materials, general labouring and supervision.

3   *Cost of services.* These will comprise the costs of providing the essential services to production, for example, inspection, stores, and general maintenance.

4   *Administration costs.* These may include such functions as production engineering, production planning and control, general works administration and, if they come under the jurisdiction of the production function, purchasing and personnel management.

5   *Expenses.* It is fairly common to show the basic cost elements as a first step in developing cost control and product costs. In this case (1) to (4) above would com-

prise salaries and wages only and expenses would be
shown together in section (5) of the statement. The
procedure will be clarified in examples that follow later.
It is essential to relate production costs to productivity. The
basic elements of production costs have been outlined and it
is, therefore, necessary to consider the measurement of productivity. Before doing so, however, it may be appropriate to
consider first the systems of costing in general use.

9.3   Costing systems

Costing systems are generally developed to suit the type of
production and this can be largely governed by the product
and the volume of output.

In the process industry it is customary, for example, to
operate process costing. In the engineering industry it may
be job costing, batch costing or, where there is mass production on the flow principle, a system specially developed for
the purpose. Many costing systems are adaptations of one or
the other of these two basic systems.

In the process costing of a homogeneous product where
the raw materials are fed into the system and moved automatically through a series of operations until they emerge as
the finished product, it is usual to prepare a period cost
statement. A summary of the raw materials cost is made. The
operating costs are analysed under a number of cost headings
and related to the output obtained. The total cost is usually
expressed as a cost per unit of output which may also be compared with the standard cost, if a standard costing system
exists.

Alternatively, where the product is processed in batches it
is more usual to list the operations contained in the total
process and to show the cost of each operation to arrive at
the total cost.

In the costing of engineering products the treatment of
operating costs is not so straightforward. The method most
commonly applied is to subdivide the operating costs into
direct labour and overheads. The overhead cost is usually
applied as a percentage of the direct labour cost or as a rate

per labour hour. One percentage or rate may be applied for the factory as a whole or they may be calculated for each production department or production centre. A group of similar machines may be treated as a production centre.

In determining the operating costs particular to a job, batch or product it is only necessary to know the labour cost in total or by departments or production centres, according to the method used, to apply the appropriate overhead percentages to arrive at the overheads cost. Where overheads are applied as a rate per labour hour then the hours as well as the labour cost must be known.

Another method in common use in engineering costing is to calculate a rate per production hour for each production centre in respect of operating costs. Figure 9.1 provides an outline of this procedure.

For the purpose of the illustration five production centres are shown and these may be production departments and/or machine groups. The standard hours budgeted for each production centre are shown. Here it has to be mentioned that a standard hour represents a unit of work as determined by work study. Where it is not practicable to establish standard hours then a forecast of actual production hours may be used. In either case the forecast will be based on the number of production operators to be employed.

Figure 9.1 shows the budgeted costs for the production centres. Some of these costs are directly incurred by production centres, while others are general to all centres and have to be apportioned to each on the basis of knowledge and judgement.

The costs of the production departments will normally be incurred directly but most of the other costs have to be shared. The costs shown in the indirect or functional departments are in respect of salaries and wages; all expenses are shown under the two headings of partly variable and fixed. The total expenditure shown against each production centre dividend by the hours, standard or actual, for the centre gives the hourly rate.

Costing concepts also influence the application of the basic costing systems. First there is the absorption costing system, sometimes termed a full costing system. This may

PARTICULARS	1	2	3	4	5	TOTAL
Period _____						
Standard hours (B)						
	£	£	£	£	£	£
Production centres						
Production direct labour						
Production indirect labour						
Holiday and sickness pay						
Indirect wages						
Supervision						
TOTAL						
Auxiliary departments						
Maintenance salaries and wages						
Toolroom salaries and wages						
Stores salaries and wages						
Inspection (shop) salaries and wages						
TOTAL						
Services and administration						
Production engineering salaries						
Production control salaries						
Purchasing department salaries						
Personnel department salaries						
Works administration salaries						
TOTAL						
Expenses (partly variable)						
Consumable stores						
Loose tools						
Maintenance materials						
Power						
General factory expenses						
Training expenses						
Allocated expenses						
TOTAL						
Fixed expenses						
Depreciation plant and tools						
Depreciation fixtures and fittings						
Establishment charges						
TOTAL						
TOTAL EXPENDITURE						
RATE PER STANDARD HOUR						

Figure 9.1   Annual production budget

still be regarded as the conventional costing system and is the one illustrated in Figure 9.1. In this system all the operating costs are taken into account in establishing the rate for each production centre. Consequently the total operating costs are chargeable to products.

In marginal costing systems only those operating costs that are variable in relation to changes in the volume of output are included in the rates and in the product costs. The fixed costs are written off in the period profit and loss statements.

In standard costing, predetermined product costs are established for the products based on reasonable standards of performance. Variances between actual and standard costs indicate the efficiency of operation and enable management to concentrate on the exceptions and the reasons for them.

There is another device that business men have been applying for many years. This has been termed marginal costs or marginal costing. It is not a distinctive system and should not be confused with marginal costing systems which were developed many years later. The definition of a marginal cost in this connection is 'the additional cost that would be incurred to produce an additional unit of output'. It is usually applied where there is surplus production capacity. It operates on the principle that the current operating level has to absorb all the fixed costs and that if additional orders can be obtained at prices that will cover the variable costs or 'out of pocket' expenses and make a contribution to fixed costs then the profits of the business will be increased.

In recent years managements have entered into productivity deals with employees. There has also been growing concern about the productivity of companies and the need to improve it. Many ideas have emerged for the measurement of productivity including productivity costing. It is reasonably certain that productivity costing will have a greater application in the future and will be an important consideration in budgeting.

Production is not a measure of productivity as an increase may be obtained through an increase in the resources. Production must be related to the costs directly associated with it to measure productivity.

It has been noted that in Figure 9.1 the operating costs for each production centre have been divided by the standard hours to determine a rate per hour for the centre. But the rate combines direct and indirect costs. If the costs directly associated with production were segregated and divided by the relative production hours then a rate per hour could be obtained for each production centre for productivity costing. But the matter does not rest there as the indirect costs have to be charged to products. The process applied to the direct costs has to be repeated for the indirect costs, which simply means that two rates have to be ascertained for each production centre. Productivity costing is discussed in detail later in the chapter.

Figure 9.2 shows the costs directly associated with a production centre comprising a number of similar machines.

Number of machines	Group number	Description	Floor space	Horse power
PRODUCTION COST			Normal volume £	Budgeted volume £
Wages				
Production operators				
Machine setters				
Machine costs				
Depreciation				
Maintenance materials				
Maintenance labour				
Power				
Tools				
Establishment charges				
Miscellaneous expenses				
TOTAL PRODUCTION COST				
COST PER STANDARD HOUR				
Operating hours				
Total working hours in the year				
less setting time				
less breakdowns, idle time, etc.				
TOTAL OPERATING HOURS				
TOTAL STANDARD HOURS				

Figure 9.2   Machine hour rate: production cost per standard hour

9.4 Measuring productivity

There are generally three conditions that have to be considered in the measurement of productivity. First, there is the condition where the output produced can be accepted as a measure of productivity. This applies particularly to the homogeneous product processed in a plant specially designed for it. In fact it generally applies to most products in process manufacture.

Secondly, there are the conditions where the output of finished products may not necessarily measure productivity but where the fluctuations in work in progress between the beginning and the end of the period are so small in relation to the total output for the period that output can be accepted as productivity. This applies particularly where the production cycle is short and the work flow is continuous. The number of cars coming off the assembly line can measure productivity. In the manufacture of clothing, for example, shirts which involve cutting, sewing and finishing the cycle is so short that output is a fair measure of productivity.

There are tremendous advantages in being able to associate output with productivity because it provides a simple measure and effective control both from the viewpoint of production planning and costing.

There is the third condition where it is virtually impossible and misleading to identify productivity with output. This applies particularly to the batch manufacture of engineering assembly products. Here the production in the feeder departments has to be related to economic batch sizes and this consideration governs output. Because the number of parts and the operaticns to be performed on them greatly exceed the number of machines, queuing time is involved. Manufactured parts are stocked in the finished parts stores until required for assembly usually on a max-min stock basis. It follows that there are too many variations involved to accept the finished output as a measure of productivity. The production cycle time in general tends to average around two months. In this type of manufacture productivity has to be measured synthetically and the basis generally adopted is the standard hour which is a unit of work as determined by work study. The measurement of productivity on the basis of standard hours generally centres on the productive operator but it can also be applied to machine performance as distinct from operator performance.

It is a fairly common practice to prepare a weekly operating statement for each production department by analysing and summarising the job cards relating to the operators. The form of these statements can vary but the general purpose is to control the utilisation and performance of the productive labour force. The weekly operating statement shown in Figure 9.3 illustrates the procedure.

The factors to be considered are utilisation, operator performance and productivity. If there are, say, 60 operators in a department then the figures shown will be a summary. Essentially productive operators are employed to do productive work. They may be usefully employed on work other than productive but this does not serve the purpose of their employment. The number of hours occupied on productive work in relation to their total attendance hours measures utilisation. The next phase is to measure the performance of the operators while employed on productive work. The measure is to compare the standard hours produced against the hours taken. This demands an allowed time for each job as fixed by work study. The final phase is to measure productivity which really combines the utilisation factor and the performance factor. To be more precise, the standard hours produced related to the attendance hours measure productivity. Where the operators spend time on productive jobs where no allowed times have been fixed, i.e. on unmeasured jobs, it is usual to add this time to the standard hours produced in measuring productivity.

The weekly operating statement is a most important statement for influencing and controlling productivity. When first introduced into a company it invariably increases productivity.

A statement (as in Figure 9.3) is prepared for each production department or each production centre. The budget is shown on the first line and thereafter the actual figures for a period of thirteen weeks. At the end of the thirteenth week totals are struck and a weekly average obtained. This form is

Week number	Number of operators	Analysis of attendance hours					Performance					Productivity
		Production hours	Re-work hours	Indirect work hours	Lost time hours	Atten-dance hours	%	Unmeasured jobs hours	Measured jobs hours	Allowed hours	%	
1	2	3	4	5	6	7	8	9	10	11	12	13
Budget												
1												
2												
3												
4												
5												
6												
7												
8												
9												
10												
11												
12												
13												
TOTAL												
WEEKLY AVERAGE												

Figure 9.3 Weekly operating statement: productive operators utilisation of attendence hours and productivity

intended to operate in conjunction with a quarterly production budget but it can be applied independently.

The statement is simple in concept:

1   *Utilisation of attendance hours:* the attendance hours of the productive operators are analysed under the headings shown (columns 3 to 7). The production hours related to the total attendance hours measure the utilisation which is shown as a percentage in column 8.

2   *Operator performance:* this measures the performance of the productive operators while working on production jobs. Unmeasured jobs are those for which allowed times have not been fixed. Measured job hours are the time spent by productive operators on jobs that have been rated by work study (column 10) and allowed hours are the equivalent time earned (column 11). The percentage in column 12 shows performance obtained as follows:

$$\frac{\text{Allowed hours (11)}}{\text{Measured job hours (10)}} \times 100\%$$

3   *Productivity:* this measures the combined effect of utilisation and operator performance and is obtained as follows:

$$\frac{\text{Allowed hours (11)}}{\text{Unmeasured (9) + measured (10) job hours}} \times 100\%$$

9.5   Evaluating productivity

In recent years some thought and discussion have been given to the question of compensating workers for an increase in productivity. This could well be a consideration of increasing importance in the future.

This involves two factors: how to measure productivity and how to assess labour's contribution. It is important that productivity should be defined in a manner acceptable to all concerned as it is a fair way, cost of living payments apart, to compensate labour for an increase in output and to create the right balance between additional profit and additional wages.

The problem in many industries is how to measure productivity. In process manufacture productivity can generally be assessed in terms of physical units and the same is largely true in continuous or mass production. There are, however, many industries manufacturing a wide range of product that cannot measure productivity in positive terms at least in the short term period and the batch manufacture of engineering products is a good example. The substitution of standard hours as a measure of productivity bridges this gap.

Productivity can best be illustrated by considering the two extremes: the first example is concerned with a natural unit of output and the second with the application of standard hours.

In both cases the direct production costs are based on the annual budget.

A chemical company produces a single product in a plant specially designed for the purpose. It prepares a four-weekly statement (see Figure 9.4) and relates output to direct production costs to measure productivity. In the statement below the budget figures are shown in the first column and the actual figures for the first four weeks of the financial year in the second column. These figures are an over-simplification to illustrate the principle, but it illustrates the principle involved in more complex situations.

	Budget	Actual
Output, tons	1000	1250
Direct production costs:		
Wages and salaries		
Plant costs		
Establishment charges		
Other expenses		
TOTAL	£200000	£210000
Cost per ton	£200	£168

Productivity is calculated as follows:

$$\frac{\text{Actual output} \times \text{Budget cost per ton}}{\text{Direct production costs}} \times 100$$

$$= \frac{1250 \times £200 \times 100}{£210000} = 119\%$$

Figure 9.4   Four-weekly operating statement

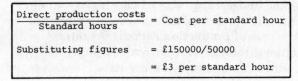

```
Direct production costs
────────────────────────  = Cost per standard hour
     Standard hours

Substituting figures     = £150000/50000

                         = £3 per standard hour
```

Figure 9.5   Cost per standard hour calculation

The next example shows the application of these principles where standard hours are the only measure of productivity. Where production is machine-orientated it is the general practice to establish figures for each group of similar machines but where labour is the predominant factor and machines are few and simple then figures are usually determined in terms of each production department. The figures shown in Figure 9.5 can relate to a group of machines or to a production department.

In preparing the production cost budget a cost per standard hour is developed for each group of machines and each assembly section, or by production departments as the case may be. The procedure as touched on earlier is:

1 To budget the standard hours required from each machine group of department.
2 To identify the direct production costs associated with production. These have been mentioned previously.
3 To budget the direct costs of production for each machine group or department.
4 To evaluate the direct cost rate for each machine group or department by dividing the direct production costs by the standard hours.

In formulating a production cost budget, or any other budget, two factors are always present; ensuring the accuracy of the figures and providing the means for checking performance against budget to measure achievement. The procedure is illustrated in an abbreviated form in Figures 9.6 and 9.7 to show the comparison of actual against budget.

A number of points have to be noted about this example. It purports to be the actual performance for the first four weeks of the year to which the budget relates. In this example there is only one link with the annual budget but it is a very important link. The rates per standard hour are those fixed by the annual budget; the two variables in actual performance are the hours produced and the direct production costs. Where the value of production exceeds the direct costs of production it represents an increase in productivity against budget which can be simply expressed as shown in Figure 9.7.

Productivity has been measured by relating the value of production to the direct costs of production. It has been based on the standard hours produced multiplied by the rates per standard hour as fixed by the annual budget. Productivity can improve not because of an increase in output but through a reduction in costs. It is feasible, for example, that output may be maintained with a smaller labour force. This may not satisfy a company where there is a need to increase output but from the viewpoint of the workers this represents an increase in productivity.

Much stress has been laid on standard hours which are measured units of work. Setting standard hours demands work study. Where this is not practical the estimated hours spent on production jobs can be substituted.

9.6   The production cost budget

In the modern setting with mechanisation and automation occupying a major role the subdivision of production costs into direct labour cost and overheads which has been the general practice for many years is losing much of its original purpose and value. Where expensive machines are involved the machine hour is assuming more importance than the direct labour hour. The tendency will be to regard production costs as production operating costs and to subdivide these into direct operating costs and indirect operating costs. The direct operating cost will include all factors which directly influence output and productivity; the indirect operating costs will be in respect of the supporting activities.

The first approach to the cost budget is the classification of expenditure. It is important that expenses should be clearly defined to indicate the nature of the expense. The classification should be reasonably comprehensive without being too

Machine group or department	Standard hours produced, £	Rate per standard hour, £	Value of production, £
A	10,000	3.00	30,000
B	20,000	4.00	80,000
C	15,000	3.00	45,000
D	12,000	5.00	60,000
TOTAL	57,000		215,000

Figure 9.6   Four-weekly statement: value of production

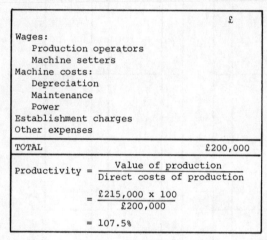

	£

Wages:
    Production operators
    Machine setters
Machine costs:
    Depreciation
    Maintenance
    Power
Establishment charges
Other expenses	

TOTAL	£200,000

$$\text{Productivity} = \frac{\text{Value of production}}{\text{Direct costs of production}}$$

$$= \frac{\pounds 215{,}000 \times 100}{\pounds 200{,}000}$$

$$= 107.5\%$$

Figure 9.7   Four-weekly statement: direct production costs

detailed. Needless to say the form of presentation and the extent of the analysis of expenses can vary between companies.

It may be appropriate at this point to refer to the production operating costs as the direct costs of production as incurred by the production centres and the 'added costs' as representing the costs of operating the indirect departments.

Once the annual production budget has been finalised in terms of the quantity of each product that has to be produced the operating cost budget has to be developed by stages (see Figures 9.8 — 9.11)

PRODUCTION CENTRES	1	2	3	4	5	TOTAL
Product Quantity	Standard hours	Standard hours	Standard hours	Standard hours	Standard hours	Standard hours
A						
B						
C						
D						
E						
TOTAL						

Figure 9.8   Annual budget: production output in standard hours

PRODUCTION CENTRES	1	2	3	4	5	TOTAL
Standard hours (1)						
Equivalent production hours						
Add for production indirect						
TOTAL ATTENDANCE HOURS						
Annual attendance hours per operator						
Number of operators						

Figure 9.9   Annual budget: productive operators

PRODUCTIVITY AND DIRECT OPERATING COST

Period _____

	Year to date				This period			
	Budget		Actual		Budget		Actual	
	£	%	£	%	£	%	£	%
Standard hours produced								
Value of production (budget rates)	100.0				100.0			100.0
Direct operating costs:								
Direct labour cost								
Indirect labour cost								
Other wages								
Holidays and sickness pay								
Depreciation plant and machinery								
Maintenance plant and machinery								
Power								
Sundry supplies								
General expenses								
Establishment charges								
TOTAL DIRECT OPERATING COSTS								
Operating variance (gain or loss)								

Figure 9.10 Productivity and direct operating cost

9.6.1   Stage 1 (Figure 9.8)

This shows the standard hours required in each production centre to manufacture the budgeted quantity of each product and the aggregate standard hours. The production centre may be a group of similar machines or a department. Standard times have been established by work study for all operations for every product and it is a simple matter to collate this information. This lends itself to computer application.

9.6.2   Stage 2 (Figure 9.9)

This shows the procedure for deciding the number of productive operators required. The total standard hours in Stage 1 are repeated in Stage 2. The standard hours have to be reduced to actual hours by applying a performance factor. If, for example, 100 standard hours can be produced in 80 actual hours then the total standard hours multiplied by 0.08 will give the equivalent production hours. It has to be noted too that a productive operator will not be occupied the whole of his time on productive work. Interferences and delays occur and waiting time cannot be completely eliminated. On average productive work accounts for no more, and frequently less, than 95 per cent of the time of the operator. If this figure is acceptable the equivalent production hours have to be increased in the ratio of 100 to 95 to arrive at the total. Attendance hours of an operator will be based on the number of working days in the year (less allowance for sickness) and the average working hours per day. The total attendance hours divided by the annual attendance hours per operator will give the number of operators required in total and for each production centre. The final step is to determine the grades of the operators; male or female, skilled or semi-skilled, etc.

Figure 9.11   Productivity and added cost ⟶

PRODUCTIVITY AND ADDED COST

Period _____

	Year to date				This period			
	Budget		Actual		Budget		Actual	
	£	%	£	%	£	%	£	%
Standard hours produced	100.0				100.0			
Value of added costs (budget rates)		100.0						100.0
OPERATING COSTS (INDIRECT)								
SALARIES AND WAGES:								
1 Production departments (direct)								
2 Auxiliary departments:								
Maintenance (general)								
Stores								
Inspection								
TOTAL AUXILIARY DEPARTMENTS								
3 Services and administration:								
Personnel department								
Production engineering								
Production planning and control								
Purchasing								
Administration								
TOTAL SERVICES AND ADMINISTRATION								
TOTAL SALARIES AND WAGES								
EXPENSES								
Consumable materials								
Loose tools								
Printing and stationery								
Training expenses								
Repairs to plant (general)								
Depreciation (general)								
Establishment charges								
TOTAL EXPENSES								
TOTAL OPERATING COSTS								
Variance (gain or loss)								

9.6.3   Stage 3 (Figures 9.10 and 9.11)

This stage is the preparation of the operating cost budget. This has to be considered and illustrated in steps. The first step is concentrated on the production department. The direct costs of production are defined and established in terms of machine groups in a department or for the department as a whole, dependent upon the requirements of the management. The second step is to establish the costs of each production department that have not been absorbed by the direct costs of production, what may be termed production indirect costs. The third step is to consider the other departments that are contained in the production operating function. These are generally classed as the indirect departments and for convenience are subdivided into two groups — the auxiliary departments and the services and administration departments.

The procedure is illustrated in the following subdivisions:

1   Productivity and the direct costs of production (Figure 9.10)
2   Added costs which include salaries and wages grouped into production departments, indirect, auxiliary departments and services and administration departments, and expenses which exclude, of course, any that are charged in the direct production costs (Figure 9.11).

In framing the budget for the production operating costs the necessary controls for measuring performance and the information required for establishing product costs have to be considered.

The forms illustrated in Figures 9.10 and 9.11 can be used for the annual budget and also for comparing actual performance with budget each period on a monthly, or perhaps four-weekly basis. In the annual budget all the direct and indirect costs, salaries, wages and expenses, are shown as percentages of the total value of production. The same procedure is applied in the period statements. Percentages have the advantage of highlighting variances.

As previously stated in preparing the annual budget the direct production costs and the standard hours obtainable are budgeted for each production centre. These are summarised to arrive at the total costs and total standard hours. In fact it is the budgeted total cost that represents the value of production. The other figure that has to be established is the direct production cost per standard hour for each production centre.

In preparing period statements the standard hours produced by each production centre are multiplied by the budgeted cost per standard hour for that centre. A summary of the values for each centre gives the total value of production for the period. The total costs of direct production for the period compared with the total evaluated production gives the gain or loss for the period. It will be noted that the actual direct production costs for the period can be established in total without the need to establish them for each production centre.

The details shown in Figures 9.10 and 9.11 do not claim to be exhaustive. Companies sometimes like to analyse expenditure in greater detail.

Where all the divisions of a business are sited together, which is the position with most companies, then the establishment charges will probably embrace all the divisions and will have to be allocated to each on the relative space occupied. The charges for the production division will be subdivided to show the amount to be included in the direct production costs and the balance to be shown under expenses indirect.

9.7 The allocation of 'added costs'

The need to establish a budgeted cost per standard hour for the direct operating or production costs of each production centre has been discussed. It is also necessary to establish a rate per standard hour for each production centre for added costs. The charges to each indirect department for salaries and wages are known and these have to be increased by an appropriate share of the general expenses to arrive at the total cost of each indirect department. A typical example of a prorated expense is establishment charges which will be allocated to each indirect department according to the space occupied. Once the total cost of each indirect department has been established this will be allocated to each production centre. The allocation may be based on an assessment or according to the number of productive operators employed in the production centre or other satisfactory basis. Production planning, for example, will probably be allocated according to the number of productive operators in each production centre.

The budgeted cost rates to be established follow the lines shown in Figure 9.12. These cost rates are required for establishing product costs and for control purposes. The rates remain unchanged throughout the year of the budget. This presumes that the budget will not be revised in the course of the year, a practice that is being adopted by an increasing number of companies, particularly where short term production budgeting is applied.

9.8   Detailed considerations

It has been shown that Figures 9.10 and 9.11 together constitute the budget for production operating costs. Certain details have to be added to complete the procedure.

9.8.1   Productivity and direct operating costs (Figure 9.10)

As previously stated this form serves two purposes — to show the annual budget and to periodically compare the actual results against the budget.

The value of production was ascertained by stages; the direct costs of production and the standard hours obtainable were established by production centres and a cost rate per standard hour ascertained for each centre. A summary of the direct production costs for the various centres gave the total value of production.

From the viewpoint of preparing an annual budget it would have been sufficient and simpler to have established the direct operating costs in total without segregating into production centres but a rate per standard hour for each centre is essential for three purposes:

Production centre	DIRECT COSTS			ADDED COSTS	
	Budgeted standard hours	Budgeted direct operating costs, £	Rate per standard hour, £	Budgeted added costs, £	Rate per standard hour, £
A B C etc.					

Figure 9.12

1   To establish product costs on a reliable basis.
2   To compare actual performance against budget.
3   To prepare short term production budgets.

The various costs shown on this statement are in the main self-explanatory. The wages of the operators include payments by the company on behalf of employees in accordance with statutory obligations, for example, national health insurance. Direct labour cost represents the time spent by operators on productive work. The production indirect labour cost represents lost time of productive operators and/ or time spent on non-productive jobs.

9.8.2   *Productivity and added costs (Figure 9.11)*

Added costs include the indirect work done in the production departments, for example, clerical, supervision and labouring and the costs of operating the indirect departments which have been analysed under the headings of auxiliary, services and administration and expenses. It is necessary to allocate these indirect costs to the various production centres in accordance with the services rendered and to establish an added cost rate per standard hour for each centre. It should be mentioned that salaries and wages include contributions by employers and holiday and sickness pay. Expenses exclude amounts charged in the direct costs.

9.9   Comparison of actual and budgeted performance

Every month or four-weekly period actual performance will be measured against the budget and the variances and the reasons for them analysed. The annual budget will be subdivided into working days in the year and related to the number of working days in each period.

    The first and probably the most important comparison is the value of production and as a further consideration the number of standard hours produced. This comparison is shown in Figure 9.10.

    Where actual value of production or productivity is in line

with budget then the costs will be compared to highlight variances. Where productivity varies to any extent then a straightforward comparison of costs could be misleading in view of the fixed and variable elements. This is where the short term production budget performs a useful function as discussed later.

Where actual productivity varies against budget it is important to note that the column shown as 'actual' on the statement has its own built-in controls both with regard to productivity and direct operating costs (Figure 9.10) and to productivity and added costs (Figure 9.11). It has been shown previously that 'actual' productivity is evaluated by the standard hours produced in the period by that centre and aggregating the values for all production centres. The comparison, therefore, is actual production evaluated at budgeted rates compared with actual production at the actual costs incurred. The difference between these two values constitutes the variance. There should be a favourable variance when actual productivity exceeds budget or an unfavourable variance when the situation is reversed.

The same remarks apply to added costs and the procedure follows the same lines by applying the standard hours for each production centre to the budgeted rate for added costs appropriate to that centre. Here again a variance is established.

It will be noted that the procedure to be followed in establishing the actual figures each period is comparatively simple.

1   Productivity and direct operating costs (Figure 9.10):
    a   Evaluate the standard hours produced at budgeted rates.
    b   Show the amount incurred against each cost item.
    c   Establish the variance.
2   Productivity and added costs (Figure 9.11):
    a   Evaluate the standard hours at the budgeted rates for added costs.
    b   Show the salaries and wages incurred against each department listed.
    c   Show the amount incurred against each item of expense.

d   Add *b* and *c* and compare with *a* to establish the
variance.

9.10   The short-term production budget

Some companies accept the annual budget as an operational
programme for all divisions of the business. Other companies,
probably the majority, accept the annual budget as an operational programme for all divisions with the exception of the
production divisions. In these instances the annual production budget provides the means for establishing the profit
expectations of the company but its function ends there.

An operational budget has to be related to the span of
production control and to the period where the production
division has complete jurisdiction over its operations. Where
a company produces standard products the period represented
by production programming will normally decide the period
of the short-term production budget. If the company makes
non-standard products or standard products modified to
customer requirements the budget period will be influenced
by the normal period covered by the order book. In general
the budget period should not be less than three months. A
shorter period is less likely to influence the results.

A short-term budget is prepared on exactly the same lines
as for the actual figures in the period statement except that
the figures are budgeted and not actual. The rates per
standard hour established in the annual budget for each
production centre in respect to direct operating costs and
added costs are applied in the short-term budget to the budgeted standard hours.

It may well be asked what advantages there are in a short-
term budget that uses rates established by an annual budget
for evaluating productivity. The answer is that the short-
term budget eliminates speculation. It projects an attainable
productivity and the costs associated with it in contradiction
to potential productivity and related costs as projected by
the annual budget.

The short-term budget performs an important function in
its own right; it projects the standard hours to be produced

by each production centre and the direct operating costs and added costs that will be incurred. These projections relate to a production programme that is within the control of the production division. Once the short term budget is approved it carries with it accountability for performance. To take a case in point one company prepares four quarterly budgets to operate in parallel with the annual budget. The production division is not held responsible for the annual budget but it is accountable for performance against the quarterly budgets.

The short-term budget supplements the annual budget. The primary aim of management is to realise the profit potential projected by the annual budget. It must be aware of any factors that adversely affect the profit and preferably be forewarned and the short-term budget does this through projecting the variances ahead of events. The short-term budget can influence management decisions. For example if it projects a lower level of production due to fluctuations in the order book management may be prepared to manufacture for stock for the duration of the budget to maintain normal output.

9.11 Other considerations

The rates established by the annual production budget for each production centre in relation to direct operating costs and added costs provide the basis for establishing product costs. These rates are also used for evaluating work-in-progress and stock. These will be considered in detail in the chapter on management accounting.

9.12 Cost inflation

Until recently cost inflation could be measured with a fair degree of accuracy for budget purposes. But in the last two years or thereabouts inflation has reached unparalleled levels not likely to be foreseen by the majority of companies. A fair degree of accuracy in budgeting is implicit in productivity costing.

In the discussion in productivity costing it was noted that production had to be related to costs as a means of measuring productivity. The basis for evaluating production was provided by the rates established through the annual budget. Any significant shift in the budget through unprecedented cost inflation weakens, if it does not invalidate, productivity costing.

Any company that operates short-term production budgets in parallel with the annual budget, for example, quarterly budgets has a certain advantage inasmuch as its cost projections are subject to review at frequent intervals.

Every time a quarterly budget is prepared the production that can be reasonably expected is evaluated at the rates established by the annual budget. Costs are assessed in relation to current conditions and outlook. The difference between the value of production and the cost of production represents a variance, favourable or unfavourable. This is regarded, once the budget has been approved, as an uncontrollable variance. Only when the actual variance exceeds the uncontrollable variance is performance investigated. This investigation must have regard to the possible effects of inflation.

Viewed from a general standpoint variances may arise from increased usage or increased costs arising from inflation or a combination of both. Until inflation can be contained at predictable levels it may be necessary for a company to analyse the variances to determine the effect of inflation.

9.13   Summary

A production budget is generally an extension of the sales budget, subject to any increase in inventories that may be decided.

The sales budget has, of course, to provide a balanced production mix that will largely utilise the production capacity and permit economic production. Indeed a sales budget will not generally be acceptable unless it satisfies these conditions.

There has to be a clear understanding on the purpose of an

annual budget. Its object is to identify and evaluate those factors which will have a major impact on operations during the coming year. It is an assessment of opportunities and difficulties against the background of competition and market conditions. A company must evaluate its expectations and plan its operations to achieve them. A budget that is based on comprehensive information and a factual approach permits management to plan the operations of the business to maximise profit. In this connection it has to be appreciated that better information promotes better management. Actual performance has to be measured against budget at frequent intervals, monthly or four-weekly, to check the progress being made. Deviations, if any, have to be reassessed in relation to their effect on the annual budgeted profit. Reasons for them have to be established and corrective action taken. This sums up the purpose of an annual budget.

A criticism often made about an annual budget is that it measures costs at one level of output only and in the event of any deviation it provides no means of controlling them. In this connection it has to be appreciated that a budget is not only concerned with costs but also with income and in many cases the latter can be more important. But to deal with the question an annual budget is not concerned with the measurement of costs at various levels of output. This control can be exercised through a supplementary procedure, for example, through a flexible budget. In more recent years short-term production budgets have been introduced for this purpose.

A flexible budget measures cost variances after the event. The short-term production budget controls output as well as costs and it shows the probable results before the event in time for management action. The period of the short-term budget is important. It must cover the period during which the production division has complete control over its operations and can be held accountable for the performance achieved. Some companies budget production on a monthly basis but when this procedure is examined it is generally an accounting device as it is too short a period for management to influence the results. A quarterly budget is usually practical for management purposes.

Particular emphasis has been given to productivity costing

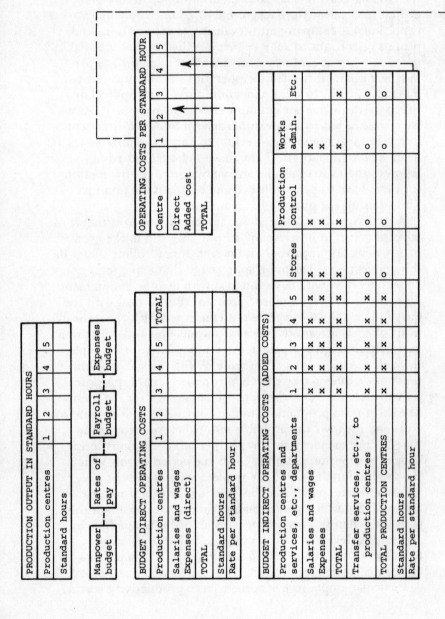

PRODUCTION OUTPUT IN STANDARD HOURS

Production centres	1	2	3	4	5
Standard hours					

Manpower budget --- Rates of pay --- Payroll budget --- Expenses budget

BUDGET DIRECT OPERATING COSTS

Production centres	1	2	3	4	5	TOTAL
Salaries and wages						
Expenses (direct)						
TOTAL						
Standard hours						
Rate per standard hour						

OPERATING COSTS PER STANDARD HOUR

Centre	1	2	3	4	5
Direct					
Added cost					
TOTAL					

BUDGET INDIRECT OPERATING COSTS (ADDED COSTS)

Production centres and services, etc., departments	1	2	3	4	5	Stores	Production control	Works admin.	Etc.
Salaries and wages	x	x	x	x	x	x	x	x	
Expenses	x	x	x	x	x	x	x	x	x
TOTAL	x	x	x	x	x	x	x	x	
Transfer services, etc., to production centres	x	x	x	x	x	o	o	o	o
TOTAL PRODUCTION CENTRES	x	x	x	x	x	o	o	o	o
Standard hours									
Rate per standard hour									

COMPARISON OF ACTUAL AND BUDGET

Production centres	1	2	3	4	5	TOTAL
Standard hours produced						
Value of production						
Value of added costs						

Budgeted rates

MONTHLY COST COMPARISON	Month	
	Budget, £	Actual, £
1 Value of production		
2 Direct operating costs:		
Salaries and wages		
Expenses		
TOTAL		
Variance (1 – 2): gain or loss		
1 Value of added costs		
2 Indirect operating costs:		
Salaries and wages		
Expenses		
TOTAL		
Variance (1 – 2): gain or loss		

QUARTERLY BUDGET

Production centres	1	2	3	4	5	TOTAL
Budgeted standard hours						
Value of production						
Value of added costs						

QUARTERLY BUDGET	£
1 Value of production	
2 Direct operating costs:	
Salaries and wages	
Expenses	
TOTAL	
Variance (1 – 2): gain or loss	
1 Value of added costs	
2 Indirect operating costs:	
Salaries and wages	
Expenses	
TOTAL	
Variance (1 – 2): gain or loss	

Figure 9.13   Annual production budget: production operating costs

for the reason that it highlights the important factors and
can provide an effective control for management purposes. A
number of methods are in common use for ascertaining and
controlling the operating costs of the production division.
Most of them are based on absorption costs, or full costs, the
main exception being marginal costing which operates on
variable expenses only. Reference has also been made to
standard costing which provides an effective measure of
actual performance. It assists management in managing
through exceptions.

It has to be appreciated that standard costing is not essential for budgeting as many companies operate effective
budgetary procedures without it.

A chart is shown in Figure 9.13 to illustrate the procedure
in productivity costing. Although a simple system it can be
confusing in the initial stages and it is important to avoid this.
To keep the chart simple expenses are not detailed, for
example, the expenses included in the direct operating costs
are simply shown as 'Expenses'. For the same reason only a
few of the indirect departments are shown to illustrate the
procedure. In practice every department is shown.

The manpower budget shows the number of persons and
the grades to be employed in each department, direct and
indirect. This is the basis for calculating the salaries and wages
payable for each department. It then remains for the expenses
to be budgeted and charged to departments. As a rule it is not
difficult to budget the amount that will be incurred for each
item of expense but few, if any, expenses are directly incurred
by departments and these have to be allocated on an assessment of usage or benefits obtained.

Once the operating costs of every department have been
established, it is necessary to transfer the costs of the indirect
departments to the productive departments. Firstly there are
the indirect costs of the production departments, labouring,
clerical and supervision and then the costs of the indirect departments. The allocation of the indirect costs has to be based
on an assessment.

The whole of this procedure is finalised by establishing two
rates for each production department, one for the direct
costs and the other for the indirect costs. The rate may be

based on the budgeted standard hours, or failing this, on the production hours.

It is important to note that these rates are established for the budget only and no further rates will be calculated until the next budget. By the same token it is only necessary to allocate the operating costs of the indirect departments to the direct departments when calculating new rates. The comparison of the actual operating costs with the budgeted costs is done in total and not by departments (see Figure 9.10 and 9.11).

The link between the budget and the actual performance is shown and also the relation of the short-term production budget to the annual budget.

10 Research, Design and Development

Where the products of a company, or its field of interest, are technologically based, then R&D is an important factor of the business. The cost of R&D is the price a company has to pay for survival or, at the other extreme, the price of leadership.

The success of a business is largely determined by finding the right answers to the questions 'what products and what markets'. The answers should be contained in two policies: the product policy and the marketing policy. These should consider and provide the answers to the implications involved. A carefully considered product policy should do much to ensure that the products are compatible with the skills and resources of the company. R&D has to operate within the framework of the products policy and the marketing strategy.

10.1 Product policy

The products of a company in conjunction with its field of interest decide the fundamental nature of the business. It is only through its products and its marketing strategy that a company can determine its customers, its markets, its competitors and the type of organisation and orientation suited to its operations. Product policies are the focal point of business strategy and a business can only be viable and progressive when it clearly sees the products and markets that will provide the required sales income during the next three to five years. A sound product policy is the starting point in building a successful business. In this connection the small business can be as efficient as the large business providing it chooses the products appropriate to its size and realises that it cannot make the variety or complexity of product that is only suited to large-scale operation. Any business can fail when it engages in a product that is too complex for its size and resources. The intensification of R&D in recent years and the mounting costs involved can cripple a company unless it has the volume of sales to support it.

10.2   R&D framework

The type of product and the size of the company obviously influence the outlook on R&D and its organisation. Another important influence is the attitude of the chief executive towards R&D. This is a function that is more vulnerable than most to a change of executive involving, perhaps, a change of attitude. The more sophisticated and progressive companies think in terms of a product philosophy. The object is to cultivate a rational approach to R&D and product planning to ensure that the company is abreast or, perhaps, ahead of competition. It is not unusual to have a products committee with representatives from all major components of the business that review and co-ordinate product planning. The basis of operation is generally through a products development programme. The programme usually lists the projects to be undertaken, the respective priorities and the approximate date for completion of the development. This programme may cover a period of five years.

   Research and product development may include all or many of the following:

1   *Basic research* aimed at enlarging the knowledge of the company generally without an immediate application in view.

2   *Applied research* which aims at obtaining knowledge with a particular purpose in view.

3   *New concepts:* innovation is important in its application to products and to the methods of production.
4   *New design:* where the aim is to design a product as a substitute for an existing product then it should be expressed through an improved or more sophisticated design.
5   *Routine design:* this follows in designing an improved product. It is important to identify what is routine to ensure that it is treated in a routine manner.
6   *Technical documentation* issued as a means of providing essential information for production.
7   *Production preparation:* this involves the plan of manufacture and providing the facilities required, and production planning including procurement of materials.

The organisation of research, design and development varies with products and companies. Where the main object is to design more sophisticated products to replace existing products, e.g. motor cars and the like, then the number of persons employed will generally be consistent over a fairly prolonged period. Where present products have to be replaced by different and, perhaps, unrelated products as can happen in the electronics field then the organisation of design and product development could be less consistent. There are companies, of course, that are prepared to spend a percentage of the sales figure on research and development and plan the organisation accordingly . They believe with a fair degree of justification that the new products resulting from this policy more than compensate them for the effort and the expenditure involved. Leading companies that are efficient in directing and controlling the R&D function regularly spend more money than their competitors on the principle that spending power promotes superiority and they are generally right.

There are companies that design and produce products to meet the specific requirements of customers. Some of these products can be complex and require advanced technology. The design and development cost is generally included in the selling price to the customer.

Everything a company does or hopes to do must be centred on its products and markets. The marketability of the products is the key to success. Products cannot be left to *ad hoc* decisions or to periodical considerations. Product design is a continuing operation and must be continuously monitored and reviewed. In a company where the life cycle of the products do not average more than five years then a product philosophy is warranted. There should be continuous efforts to advance technology and to innovate. Better information should be continuously strived for to permit better management and to give a competitive edge. Coordination of design and development are essential in view of its impact on manufacture and marketing. A products development programme is essential and this should at least span the life cycle of the existing products.

The importance and the magnitude of R&D can vary extensively according to the field of interest and to the rate and degree of technological and scientific advancement. Take the differences that can exist, for example, between aero engines, motor cars, washing machines and such products as nylon and other man-made fibres.

10.3   The life cycle of a product

Reference has been made previously to the life cycle of a product. Here the consideration is providing new products to substitute as required. Every product goes through the same stages from growth to saturation and decline. The sales decline because more sophisticated products are entering the market.

For its own protection a company must know the average life span of a product. Figure 10.1 shows the various stages in the life of a product. If each of these stages occupies a year then the total cycle is five years. The new product should overlap the existing product to avoid a break in sales or a reduction in sales. In the illustration the substitute product is shown as starting at the beginning of the third year. A company must establish a pattern or better still a product development programme.

Long-term budgeting through a series of annual budgets is important in this connection to monitor product develop-

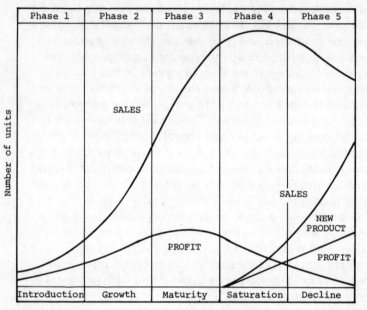

| Phase 1 | Phase 2 | Phase 3 | Phase 4 | Phase 5 |

SALES

SALES

NEW
PRODUCT

PROFIT

PROFIT

Number of units

| Introduction | Growth | Maturity | Saturation | Decline |

Figure 10.1   Product life cycle and overlapping of replacement product

ments to ensure that new products are available at the right time and in the right quantity to maintain or improve sales and profit.

10.4   New projects

New projects may arise from several sources. In many companies it can be regarded as the function of the marketing division to introduce potential projects for consideration.

In many industries projects are based on advanced designs of existing products, e.g. motor cars, refrigerators and washing machines. Here companies have the advantage of knowing how to intensify their efforts to enlarge their technical and scientific knowledge. In other industries, e.g. chemicals, the accent is on developing entirely new products and here a company has to decide and define its particular field of interest and the type of R&D projects that will best serve its purpose. It will then have to define the technological and scientific knowledge required and plan its R&D organisation on this basis. It follows that new projects will be investigated before being adopted. In some companies the marketing division has to project the annual sales for three years and the probable selling price for each project. It is then technically investigated to ascertain the probable cost of producing the product and to give an indication of any capital expenditure that may be involved in machines and tools, etc.

In considering this information a company has to decide if the annual volume of sales and the cost of these sales in conjunction with the capital involved gives a satisfactory contribution. It will compare the contribution of this project with other projects that are under consideration. Another factor that has to be taken into consideration is the man hours of the design and development department which will be committed if the project is approved. Using design time to the best advantage is an important consideration particularly if the number of projects to be considered exceeds the capacity of the department.

If the project is sanctioned it may be in terms of producing a prototype and again evaluating the project. The next phase will be to manufacture a quantity of the product for market and field tests and if these are satisfactory to decide upon a production programme.

In the consideration of some products the marketing division has not only to assess sales volume and selling prices but is frequently called upon to submit a product specification that will meet the demands of the market.

The procedure outlined will generally meet the requirements of the majority of companies but there are many variations in the procedure adopted for evaluating new projects. Where projects can involve millions of pounds then the investigation can be complex, technical and highly sophisticated.

10.5   R&D costs

The methods adopted for authorising and controlling R&D costs can vary considerably according to circumstances and the resources of a company. The methods of charging the costs incurred can also vary.

One of the simplest applications is to decide the size of the establishment, the number of persons to be employed and the incidental expenses that will be incurred to provide the necessary facilities and needs of the division. The annual budget will be prepared on this basis and it may be further decided that design and development costs should be charged against profit as incurred. It follows that all projects will be authorised with due regard to priority and the design and development time required. Projects are defined to ensure that R&D efforts are properly planned, directed and controlled and not necessarily with the object of controlling costs.

Another method that is sometimes adopted is to charge the direct costs of design and development to projects and to charge the indirect costs against profit as these are incurred. The direct costs of the project are capitalised and written off against the sales of the product over a prescribed period. In this application only the indirect costs of design and development are shown in the annual budget.

One of the methods favoured by a number of companies is to cost all projects on a job costing basis. An assessment is made of the hours that will be spent directly on projects and the total costs of the department and a rate per hour established. The cost of a project will be based on the number of hours at the rate per hour and the cost of any materials used. If capital costs are incurred for a project this is a charge to the project. A project is given a number and a cost sheet is prepared for each project. Under this procedure an annual budget is not prepared for design and development as it is presumed that all the costs will be absorbed by the projects. The money spent on projects is capitalised and written off against product sales.

Many companies finance their research, design and development projects through an appropriation of profit. The idea is that the current volume of sales should finance the development of future products. Some companies spend millions of pounds a year on development but their sales volume is so large that it represents only a small percentage of sales.

The capitalisation of project costs has an element of risk.

Large sums can be involved and if projects fail a company may suffer a substantial, and in some cases, an irreparable loss.

10.6 Classification of expenditure

R&D costs may arise from several sources. There are the salaries of personnel directly engaged in project work.

They will probably book or allocate time to projects and are regarded as direct costs. The salaries of personnel not directly engaged on projects are indirect costs.

Materials used directly on projects are charged to the project. Other materials are indirect costs. If there is an experimental workshop the cost of operating it will generally be expressed as a rate per production hour and charges to projects will be based on hours booked at the standard rate. Direct materials used will be charged directly to projects. Work done by the production departments on projects will be charged in the same manner as the workshop; the hours booked to projects by a department will be evaluated at the standard rate for the department and direct materials will be a direct charge to the project.

The costs of operating the R&D department will be analysed under direct costs and indirect costs. The direct costs will comprise the salaries of personnel directly engaged on projects and the direct materials used. The indirect costs will include salaries, indirect materials, establishment charges and other expenditure which cannot be directly related to products. The direct operating costs plus the indirect costs for a period will be related to the direct hours booked to projects for the same period and a cost per hour for the total operating costs established. The cost per hour may be established on previous figures or on an assessment.

10.7 Budget applications

Where it is the policy of a company to charge research, design and development costs against profit then it is customary to budget these costs through an annual budget. The size of the organisation will generally be carefully planned and no difficulty should be encountered in determining the costs. The incidental expenses, other than capital expenditure, to enable the organisation to operate effectively can generally be determined from past records. Establishment charges representing the cost of space, lighting, heating and insurance are easily determined. Difficulties may arise, however, in budgeting the probable usage of direct materials on projects and the involvement of production in connection with projects. Previous records should provide a guide and a company can always fix ceiling figures in the budget to ensure that the costs are being controlled.

Where the custom is to charge only the direct operating costs to projects then an annual budget will be prepared in respect of the indirect costs. Where it is the practice to charge all operating costs to projects both direct and indirect and to capitalise the costs then an annual budget will not be necessary.

10.8   The basic costs of a product

Design and development decide the materials content and the work content of a product. The volume of sales determine the amount per unit of product that will be charged for fixed expenses. Conjointly these two factors constitute the basic costs of a product. Design has not only to build market appeal into the product but it has to do this at the minimum cost.

There has to be close coordination between marketing and design to ensure that the product is designed to meet market demands and to represent value to the customer. There has to be close coordination between design and production. It is essential that components and the finished product are made to the required standards and that design should aim at simplicity of manufacture and avoid refinements that increase production costs but add nothing to the performance or the value of the product. The production division is given the opportunity to comment on the design before it is finalised but this is generally confined to particular points of difficulty in manufacture where concessions are necessary. It is only in recent years that the wider implications of design have been fully appreciated and have given rise to value engineering.

Some of the more obvious shortcomings in product design are: specifying finer limits than necessary thus adding to the number of production operations; specifying a non-standard part which has to be made specially instead of the standard part of a supplier; using a wider variety of materials and parts than necessary instead of developing fewer standards that would generally apply.

In recent years value engineering and value analysis have eliminated many of the more obvious shortcomings. Value engineering and value analysis are primarily concerned with the design and manufacture of a product and its parts and the materials that are contained in it. Ideally the design of a product should ensure that it functions properly, is styled to give customer appeal and gives maximum value at minimum cost. Similarly production engineering, which determines the method of manufacture and the tools and equipment to be used should ensure that the product is manufactured at the lowest cost within the limits imposed by the design and by the volume of production. Value engineering or analysis is, therefore, not a new technique but a systematic, disciplined and more effective approach to long established principles. All of these factors have an impact on the cost of the product.

10.9 The organisation of R&D

The organisation of R&D can be almost as varied as the products that are embraced by it. Companies producing the same products can have different approaches to R&D. The attitude of top management to R&D can have a marked effect on its application. The technological and scientific possibilities inherent in the product lines or in the field of interest of the company and the rate of change are the significant factors. The present state of the art is also important. A company has to keep pace with competition or be ahead of it and it is this factor that must determine the organisation and application of R&D. A company must comply or fall out.

The size and cost of the R&D application are the factors that largely decide the organisation. In some companies the annual cost may be measured in thousands of pounds while in others it can run into millions. At the top end of the scale the planning, directing and organising of the R&D application can be one of the most complex operations of the business. Selecting the R&D projects and effectively controlling the results can be a formidable task.

In most companies R&D will comprise basic research, applied research, design and development together with co-ordination of the manufacturing requirements to provide the essential information required. Manpower will generally be allocated to these sub-functions and the extent and nature of these operations will decide the size and calibre of the operation.

10.10   Summary

This outline of R&D has to be general because applications can vary so much between companies and in the objectives to be attained. The budgeting of R&D costs can however, be narrowed down to two major choices: writing-off the costs against profit within the financial year that these are incurred or capitalising the costs. In the case of writing-off the costs the annual budget will show the total costs to be incurred. Where the costs are capitalised an annual budget will not be necessary.

11 Management Accounting

Management accounting occupies a leading position in business for several reasons, but probably its principal contribution is that it operates in a medium of vital importance to management — income, expenditure and profit — and is a universal language that can present facts of great diversity on a comparable basis as quite often financial terms are the only means of reducing variable factors to a common denominator.

11.1 The function of accounting

Accountancy can be broadly classified under the three headings of professional accountancy, management accounting and the accounting associated with public authorities. The accountancy profession is concerned with the method or the manner of presenting accounting information both with regard to statutory requirements and standard practices that provide reliable and accurate information.

Management accounting is orientated towards providing accounting information to guide management in decision-making and directing and controlling the operations of the company. In performing its specific function management accounting has to conform, of course, to the established principles of accountancy. Accounting for public authorities is orientated towards particular requirements.

The importance of accounting information to management

increases with the size of the company. In the small business management can be informed partly through personal contact. In the larger business management is remote and has to place more reliance on accounting information. In the multi-plant company and in the large international companies management has to make decisions and direct and control operations through accounting information.

It is important at the outset to emphasise the relationship between management accounting and budgeting and to the annual budget in particular. This emphasis is necessary because of the widely held belief that budgeting is a function of management accounting. Many directors and executives of companies hold this view and operate on this understanding.

Management accounting is closely associated with every phase of budgeting in providing financial information to the heads of divisions to enable them to prepare their annual budgets. It is also a function of management accounting to submit statements periodically to the executives concerned showing actual performance against budget. The only budget responsibility of management accounting is in the accuracy of the imformation provided for budgeting and budget comparison purposes coupled, of course, with budgeting and controlling its own expenditure. Budgeting is certainly not a function of accounting.

The attitude of top management to budgeting and all forms of planning can influence the benefits to be obtained. Statements made not infrequently by influential people such as 'budgeting to be successful must have the co-operation of top management' do not help. This implies that budgeting is a function below top level and that the chief executive should see that the conditions are conducive to applying it. In fact top management is not only responsible for budgeting and the other aspects of corporate planning but these should be one of its primary and most important functions. Unless this is recognised and implemented progress will be retarded.

11.2   The function of management accounting

The normal functions of management accounting may be

broadly summarised as:

1   To provide annual and period profit and loss statements and balance sheets.
2   To evaluate the financial commitments of the company for a future period and to relate them to the funds available, actual or potential. To measure cash flow in the short term.
3   To provide comparative statements for measuring performance.
4   To aid management in developing product policies and selling price structures.
5   To provide management information for formulating business objectives.
6   To carry out special investigations and to provide information for specific purposes, e.g. marginal costs.

One of the expanding roles of management accounting is the preparation of financial statements and cost information for management decisions. Management accounting is invaluable to management in getting to know and understand the business and in determining its future prospects.

11.3   The annual budget

Reference has been made previously to certain aspects of an annual budget; at this point the object is to study it in relation to the accounting function. Strategic planning with a long-term focus should shape a business for profitable operation and growth. What can be accomplished through an annual budget is largely conditioned by this long-term planning. But there is much that an annual budget can achieve through carefully planned tactics related to the circumstances of the business and the trading conditions. It has to be appreciated that budgeting is a matter of evaluating the opportunities and organising the operations to achieve these expectations.

There follows the question of how far a company is prepared to go in accepting the annual budgets as operating plans. In general the sales budget, the R&D budget and the general administration budget are accepted as operational plans carrying full responsibility for their implementation together with accountability for performance. Many companies are not prepared, however, to accept the annual production budget as an operational plan with all the commitments this implies and this factor can have an impact on management accounting.

A criticism usually levelled at an annual production budget is that it projects costs against a fixed volume of output and if there is any variation from this point the budgeted costs are no longer relevant due to the incidence of fixed and variable expenses. For this reason some accountants advocate the use of a flexible budget to be used in conjunction with the annual budget by means of which the costs appropriate to the production level achieved — and not the budgeted costs — can be determined and related to the actual costs incurred. The flexible budget is, therefore, a means of controlling the costs incurred.

The alternative to the flexible budget is a short-term production budget which can control not only expenditure but also productivity. The duration of the short-term budget is decided by the length of the period during which the production division has complete control over its operations and can be held accountable for performance. In the manufacture of standard products this may be decided in relation to the production programming period. In non-standard products it may be based on the average period of the order book. Many companies find it suitable to operate quarterly budgets. Unless production is relatively straightforward a period of less than three months is too short generally to have any significant effect. A quarterly production budget is more sophisticated than a flexible budget as it measures and controls productivity as well as costs.

In considering the advantages of a short-term operational budget where the particular circumstances of a company do not warrant an annual operating budget it has to be appreciated that many companies plan production a year ahead on the basis of an annual budget. To them a year can be a comparatively short period particularly where the plant is fully mechanised or automated and involves a considerable investment. Here profit is dependent upon running the plant at or near total capacity.

11.4   Characteristics of production expenses

Production expenses are generally defined as all the expenses, or costs, of operating the production division, excluding production materials and direct labour. They include salaries and wages, indirect materials and expenses. None of these costs can as a rule be directly related to products.

A problem in the control of expenditure is that the total does not vary in relation to the volume of production. Direct materials, for example, tend to vary in close relationship to volume. Direct labour may be a variable cost in certain cases but agreements with certain guaranties are tending to make this a partly variable cost. Many individual expense items tend to be partly variable with fixed and variable elements. Then there is a third category where expenses tend to be fixed in relation to volume. Whether expenses are fixed, variable or partly variable cannot always be decided by the nature of the expenses as management action can be an influential factor. In some cases it might be more appropriate to regard these expenses as elastic or inelastic in relation to volume rather than variable or fixed.

Since the cost of a unit of output can vary with variations in total output it poses the question of the volume level to be used for projecting product costs. This assumes greater importance if product costs are used as a guide for fixing selling prices.

If expense could be increased or decreased in direct proportion to output then several of the current problems of management and of accountants would be simplified. In a number of companies the only expense, or cost, that really varies in direct relation to output is the cost of production materials.

11.5   Production costs

There are several methods in common use for calculating manufacturing cost of a product. The first consideration is the analysis of the manufacturing cost and probably the most common procedure is to subdivide it into production materials cost, direct labour cost and indirect costs. These indirect costs are generally referred to as factory overheads or production overheads.

The manufacturing cost of the product would appear as:

Production Materials Cost	=
Direct Labour Cost	=
Factory Overheads Cost	= _____
Total Manufacturing Cost	= _____

The materials cost and direct labour cost would be directly obtained from cost information but factory overheads cannot be directly measured in like manner and have to be calculated on an arbitrary basis. Two of the common methods of arriving at the factory overheads to be charged to a product are as a percentage of direct labour cost or as a rate per direct labour hour according to the number of hours taken. These would represent blanket rates, i.e. one percentage or one direct labour hour rate for the whole of the factory. It is more usual to establish an individual rate for each production department or centre and in this case the direct labour cost or direct labour hours would have to be analysed by departments or centres to establish the factory overheads to be charged to the product.

The percentage to be applied for factory overheads or the rate per direct labour hour can be established on actual costs, for example, on monthly basis. It is more usual, however, to make these calculations on an annual basis using budgeted or estimated costs. In establishing the budgeted or estimated overhead costs for the year the usual procedure is:

1   From the manpower budget and the number and the grades to be employed in each of the indirect departments or centres calculate salaries and wages. Calculate salaries and wages of indirect personnel in productive departments.

2   List the various expenses to be incurred in the factory and budget an amount for each, e.g. power, small tools, general expenses and indirect materials, and allocate these to all departments, direct and indirect, on some representative basis. Establishment charges would, for

example, be allocated to each department on the floor space occupied.

3   Total the costs of each indirect department and transfer to the productive departments on a representative basis. The allocation of personnel department costs would, for example, be allocated on the basis of the total employees in each productive department.

At this point the productive departments have been charged with salaries and wages of indirect operators and also the share of expenses allocated directly to them. The operating costs of the indirect departments have been transferred to the productive departments. The manpower budget showing the number and the grades to be employed in each productive department will give the wages of the productive operators. The proportion of time likely to be spent by productive operators on indirect work, or lost time will be evaluated and deducted from the total wages of the operators to arrive at the direct labour cost.

To clarify the procedure Figure 11.1 lists the various cost factors for one productive department. All costs in this example, excluding direct labour costs, are comprised in the total overheads cost. It will be noted that the total operating costs of the production division are now contained in the productive departments.

Under this procedure the allocation of costs to the productive departments is carried out once a year only unless the budget is revised. Every period the overheads recovered through production at the budgeted rates are compared with

```
DEPARTMENT A                                              £
────────────────────────────────────────────────────────────
Direct labour cost                              ──────────────

Production indirect (lost time, etc.)
Expenses directly allocated
Salaries and wages of indirect personnel
    (employed in department)
Salaries and wages of indirect departments
────────────────────────────────────────────────────────────
TOTAL OVERHEADS COST
────────────────────────────────────────────────────────────
Production hours
Rate per hour (or per cent direct labour)
```

Figure 11.1   Productive department cost factors

the total operating costs incurred and the variance, with the reason for it, established. If the overhead rates are budgeted at a rate per production hour for each department then the production hours obtained during a period from these departments evaluated at the appropriate budgeted rates gives the total value of production; this compared with the actual costs incurred gives the variance.

The method of dealing with factory overheads discussed so far may be regarded as conventional and is generally referred to as 'absorption costs'. In the chapter on the production budget productivity costing was advocated as an alternative method to give, what is believed to be, more positive control. But the productivity costing system did involve the allocation of all the costs of the indirect departments to the productive departments as in absorption costing. There is a third system that has to be considered and that is marginal costing, or as it is termed in America, direct costing (which must not be confused with productivity costing). In this system only variable costs are included in factory overheads, the fixed costs being written-off each period in the profit and loss statement. This will be referred to in a later section.

11.6   Materials cost

It is necessary to consider the materials cost of a product in more detail. In the homogeneous product the materials are generally decided on a formula for the product. In the manufacture of chemicals, for example, the laboratory may prepare the formula and yield can be a very important factor in setting standard material costs and controlling performance.

In the assembly type of product each part is virtually a complete product in itself but, except as spares, it is not saleable. Here it is usual to issue an assembly parts list showing all the parts entering into the product. Some of these parts will be purchased and these may be shown at actual purchase price or at average purchase price or on the basis of prices obtained through taking FIFO (first in first out) or LIFO (last in first out) or at standard purchase prices.

Some of the parts will be manufactured and production

engineering will probably prepare an operation layout sheet (*modus operandi*) for each part giving the material specification and the quantity to be used per piece or for a number of pieces. This material is priced at one or other of the prices mentioned above. For convenience the cost of the materials may be shown against the item on the assembly parts list.

There is the further point that some of the parts listed may in fact be sub-assemblies each consisting of a number of parts. Here it is necessary to refer to the parts list for each sub-assembly to determine the parts contained in it and if purchased or manufactured. The procedure here follows the procedure mentioned for the assembly parts list; the purchase price is shown against the item on the sub-assembly parts list or the material cost if it is a manufactured item. The amount shown against each item is summarised to obtain the total materials cost for the sub-assembly which is recorded on the assembly parts list. When this procedure has been completed for all parts and sub-assemblies the assembly parts list is summarised to obtain the total materials cost of the product.

The operation layout sheet for each manufactured part generally lists the operations to be performed in sequential order, showing against each operation the machine or machine group to be used and the allowed time.

11.7   Cost of sales

In budgeting the production cost of sales for standard products the following information is required; the quantity to be produced of each product, the materials cost, the direct labour cost and the overheads cost of each product. Multiplying these various costs by the number to be produced of the product gives the total cost for the product. Summarising the costs for each product gives the total cost for the production budget. Where the production budget provides for an increase in the inventory of finished products then in preparing the budgeted cost of sales statement these must be omitted.

A typical cost of sales statement prepared in the conventional manner would be as shown in Figure 11.2. The method of obtaining these costs has been indicated in previous sec-

	£
1 Sales	

2 Cost of sales:
   a Materials cost
   b Direct labour cost
   c Overheads cost	

TOTAL PRODUCTION COST	
3 Gross profit (1 - 2)	

Figure 11.2   Productive department cost factors

tions. In recent years there has been an increasing tendency
to develop standard costs for standard products. In calculating
the materials cost for each product it is usual to set standard
prices for every raw material and every purchased part, if any.
These standard prices are set for the budget period a short
time before. The purchasing department looks at current
prices and assesses what these would be in six months time
and fixes the standard prices accordingly. With this procedure there should be favourable variances in the first half
year of the budget and adverse variances in the second half
and these should near enough cancel out by the end of the
year.

The budgeted costs of operating the factory, or production division are absorbed by the productive departments
through direct costs and a rational allocation of the indirect
costs. The budgeted standard hours to be obtained from each
productive department, group of machines or cost centre are
related to the corresponding operational costs and a rate per
standard hour established.

The budgeted cost of each product will be ascertained as
follows:

1   Direct materials cost as already mentioned using standard
     prices.
2   Factory operating cost by ascertaining the number of
     standard hours required by each department or cost
     centre to produce one unit of product and by evaluating
     the standard hours at departmental or cost centre rates.

The budgeted cost of sales will be obtained by multiplying
the unit cost of each product by the quantity to be sold. A
summary of the costs for each product will show the total

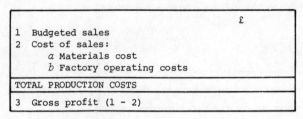

	£
1 Budgeted sales	
2 Cost of sales:	
a Materials cost	
b Factory operating costs	
TOTAL PRODUCTION COSTS	
3 Gross profit (1 - 2)	

Figure 11.3   Cost of sales budget: annual

budgeted cost. The annual cost of sales budget will appear as
shown in Figure 11.3. It is advisable in developing the standard cost of a product to include an allowance for spoilage.
This is a simple and effective method of controlling it. The
materials cost of the product is increased by an assessed
percentage. The spoilage allowance in connection with the
operating costs is expressed by adding a percentage to the
standard hours of each department or cost centre. It has to
be emphasised that spoilage allowances must be carefully
assessed to be meaningful.

In a previous chapter the productivity costing system was
discussed which divides the total operating costs of the
production division into two sections — the direct operating
costs and the added costs. In preparing a cost of sales statement the operating costs would be shown under the two
headings.

It is necessary in this context to show the cost of sales
procedure in its application to marginal costing, which may
also be termed direct costing or contributory costing.

In developing a product cost under a marginal costing
system a rate per standard hour is established as previously
described for each department, machine group or cost centre
but variable costs only are taken into account in calculating
the rate. In short the costs directly incurred by the productive
department or centre and the costs allocated to it exclude
fixed expenses which are written off to the profit and loss
statement each period.

The cost of sales would be budgeted as shown in Figure
11.4. Marginal costing is an exception to absorption costs
where all operating costs are taken into account in establishing
the hourly rates.

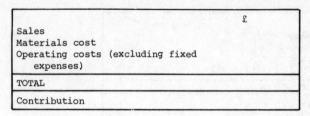

	£
Sales	
Materials cost	
Operating costs (excluding fixed expenses)	
TOTAL	
Contribution	

Figure 11.4   Cost of sales budget

In the examples quoted production hours or standard hours have been taken as a means of evaluating production in the absence of a natural unit of output. Where there is a natural unit of output this will be taken as the basis for evaluating output.

In a chemical company where the plant is specially designed to manufacture a single product the cost of sales statement would be developed on the following lines:

1   *Sales:* output for the year budgeted at average selling price per unit.
2   *Manpower budget:*
    a   The number of productive operators to be employed.
    b   The number of other personnel to be employed.
3   *Salaries and wages:* these would be derived from the manpower budget or 'headcount'.
4   *Expenses:* all expenses to be incurred would be suitably classified and an amount budgeted for each.
5   *Materials cost:* the quantity of each material to be used for the budgeted output. These materials would be evaluated at the standard prices set for the period of the budget. Yield can vary in this type of production and it is important to define the yield figure to be used in budgeting.

The cost of sales statement in a summarised form would be as shown in Figure 11.5.

11.8   Budgeting for non-standard products

In non-standard manufacture the product cannot be defined

		Tons	Per ton
1	Budgeted output		
2	Sales price per ton, £		
3	Cost of sales (production): *a* Materials cost *b* Direct operating cost *c* Added cost		
TOTAL COST OF SALES			
Gross profit (2 - 3)			

Figure 11.5   Cost of sales statement (summarised)

and this imposes certain limitations in preparing an annual budget. Sales cannot be budgeted in the conventional manner, there is no precise basis for budgeting materials costs and the application of standard hours on a work study basis is not feasible.

A company nevertheless has to assess its trading prospects for the ensuing year. Notwithstanding the difficulty of budgeting there is a real need to assess the opportunities and to plan for achieving them.

An analysis of the sales trends of the previous three years will provide useful information. Contacts with major customers through the sales representatives to learn how they view their prospects for the following year should be a useful guide. Reports on the prospects for the industry and reports from outside sources should give an indication of trading conditions. Collectively this information should give a fair indication of the trading situation; normal, favourable or adverse.

The outlook for the following year will guide a company in deciding the manpower budget. If the outlook is good and the order position strong it may budget for an increase in personnel; otherwise it will probably base the budget on its present personnel.

A company making non-standard products can establish departmental or cost centre rates for its production operating costs by any of the methods previously described except as a rate per standard hour.

There is no positive basis, however, for budgeting the materials cost or sales. One company bases its total sales on the number of budgeted production hours. It has maintained statistics over a long period to show the ratio of sales to production hours. Cost inflation can however disturb these ratios and the company increases the sales total to allow for this using the percentage increase in wage rates as a guide. Given the budgeted sales figures profit is calculated at an average percentage. By deducting all the costs and profit from sales the balance is materials cost. The ratio of materials cost to sales is checked to see if it conforms to previous experience. The annual budget may be prepared two or three times before it satisfies the budget committee.

11.9   Marginal costs and marginal costing

Brief references have been made to marginal costs in previous sections. The idea behind marginal costs is that the fixed expenses have to be absorbed by the current volume of output and if output can be increased the only additional charge incurred is the variable cost or out-of-pocket expenses. If the selling price obtainable exceeds the variable costs then total profit will be increased. Marginal costs apply where there is surplus capacity.

The marginal cost procedure mentioned above is based on conventional (full cost) systems and should not be confused with a marginal or direct costing system which is a more recent innovation.

No company should be in business to earn marginal profits on any of its products. There can be occasions however when it may be expedient to sell a product in a marginal price market or to introduce a product with a marginal profit as a temporary measure.

In the conventional costing system products are normally costed at full factory cost (including fixed expenses) and are included in stock at this amount until sold. The marginal costing system operates on a different principle in that only the variable factory costs are charged to the product and this is the value taken into stock. The fixed factory costs are charged as incurred in the profit statement for the period.

Accountants are divided on the relative merits of the two

systems. Advocates of marginal costing believe that the relative profitability of products can best be measured by deducting the variable costs from the selling price and comparing the contribution. It is debatable as to which system will best serve the purpose in particular circumstances.

Looking ahead it is difficult to see how marginal costing will maintain its present position. The trend in industry is towards an increasing investment in plant and machinery — more mechanisation and automation. In recent years there has been a growing appreciation of the need to counteract inflation and the one effective answer to this is the reduction in costs that can be achieved by producing in greater volume — the economics of large-scale production. In these conditions variable costs will be a reducing proportion of total costs and marginal costing will be measuring little more than the direct material costs. It is in this environment that productivity costing as previously described will increase in importance.

11.10   The economics of production

The economics of production largely hinges on four fundamental factors: design, volume, organisation and productivity.

11.10.1   Design

The product should be designed to satisfy the quality and price standards of the market. It should be value engineered to minimise the materials content and work content of the product. It should in particular avoid refinements that increase cost but add nothing to the value of the product.

11.10.2   Volume

Design and volume are the basic factors of product cost. There is optimum volume for a product and this should yield the lowest production cost because it permits production engineering to plan the best method of manufacture without economic restraint and to use the most appropriate production facilities.

There is also an economic volume level which may impose restraints in deciding the method of manufacture and the choice of production facilities but which permits the company to earn a viable profit. Obviously a company should aim to get closer to the optimum volume level. Where volume imposes economic restraints then the economics of the situation decide the method of manufacture as opposed to the best engineering practice.

11.10.3   Organisation

The organisation must be purposefully planned to suit the specific requirements of the business and with due regard to economy. The organisation must be strongly supported by carefully planned and comprehensive procedures to ensure efficient and economic performance. In many companies the odds are that the costs of the organisation are too high simply because personnel are not employed to the best advantage for the reason that management does not appreciate the importance of the two factors quoted; a careful study of the business to establish the organisational requirements and the value of procedures to instruct personnel on what has to be done and how it should be done.

11.10.4   Productivity

The one way to calculate and control production costs is to relate total expenditure to productivity. In process and mass, or continuous, production the output obtained is the measure of productivity. In some products, e.g. in the batch manufacture of the assembly type of engineering product, output does not measure productivity. Nevertheless it is equally important that productivity should be measured. In the absence of a natural unit of output a synthetic unit has to be adopted. The basis commonly applied is to use standard hours

as based on time study or where this is not practical the production hour. It has to be appreciated that a standard hour is
a measured unit of work as compared with a production
hour which takes no account of the operating efficiency of
the worker.

11.11   Normal activity and product costs

The effect of volume on product costs is an important factor
particularly if the costs serve as a guide to price-fixing as is
generally the case in the manufacture of non-standard products.

When a company relies on product costs as a guide to
price-fixing it should determine its normal or average level of
activity and calculate its product costs on this basis. It follows,
of couse, that prices based on normal activity should be
economic, that is the prices must be acceptable to customers
and provide a profit.

If a company operates above the normal level of activity
the product costs will be reduced since the additional output
will only incur variable or out-of-pocket expenses. If these
reduced costs are used for price-fixing then the whole of the
saving will be passed on to the customer. If, conversely, a
company has to operate below the normal activity through,
perhaps, a shortage of orders it is fairly certain that it will not
be able to increase its selling prices to recover the additional
costs per unit. The general rule, therefore, is to use product
costs at normal activity as a guide to price-fixing.

11.12   Standard costing

Standard costing was first introduced in the 1920s to provide
management with the means of exercising closer control over
production costs. A standard cost is the cost attainable when
operating at an acceptable standard of performance and at an
economic level of output. An economic level of output is one
that permits a company to earn a viable profit.

The requirement for standard costing is to establish standards such as performance level, production level and price and cost levels. The standards used in standard costing can be generally classified as (a) performance standards and (b) operational standards. Performance standards can be generally described as the performance expected in doing particular jobs or operations and operational standards as the volume of production and the expenditure appropriate to it.

Performance standards are relatively permanent in their application and have little or no concern with operating standards, for example the time allowed to perform a particular operation or the quantity of parts or product that should be obtained from a given quantity of material. Performance standards only change as a rule with the redesign of a product or changes in the method of production.

Operational standards are related to volume and can only be determined when the operational volume is decided, preferably through a budget representing the planned objective. Operational standards are subject to review and amendment every budget period. The operational volume as set by the production budget determines the materials cost and the direct and indirect operating costs of the production division. It is the formulation of these standards that makes standard costing possible. Performance standards are generally established for:

1   *Materials.* The type of materials and the quantity to be used in the manufacture of the product. This normally includes an allowance for spoilage or the standard yield expected from a given quantity of material.

2   *Production time.* This is the standard time fixed for producing a product or a number of products. In engineering products of the assembly type a standard time is fixed for each operation on every manufactured part and for the assembly of parts. The total standard time for a product includes an allowance for spoilage.

3   *Spoilage allowance.* This is the standard allowance for spoilage included in the standard cost of the product. The allowance includes materials and standard time. Spoilage is generally due to faulty workmanship but in some industries, e.g. chemicals it relates to the variation in yield obtained from a given quantity of materials.

4   *Standard batch sizes.* This is to ensure that the pro-
     duction facilities are used economically and that the
     proper relation is maintained between the preparation
     or setting time and the machine running time.
Operational standards usually comprise:
1   *The number of persons to be employed.* In total and
     subdivided by departments. The different grades of
     labour will also be classified. The 'headcount' is useful
     for the overall control of the number employed.
2   *Salary and wage rates.* These are usually determined
     from the annual budget.
3   *Standard prices.* The prices fixed by the purchasing
     department for the production materials and purchased
     parts to be used in the manufacture of the products.
     These prices are fixed just prior to the preparation of
     the annual budget and usually remain unchanged through-
     out the period of the budget.
4   *Production operating expenditure.* The amount to be
     incurred against each expense and the charge or alloca-
     tion to the departments concerned..

Standard costing can be applied without a budgeting procedure but both usually operate together. The important
function of standard costing is to measure performance
against the standards set and to establish variances in relation
to responsibilities. Variances involving standards of performance can be complicated by volume variance. Many procedures have been devised for analysing variances and some
of these are very detailed. In general sophisticated management is only interested in major factors and likes the
variances to be summarised in concrete terms, for example,
'controllable' or 'uncontrollable' variances. It is necessary,
however, to recognise what variances can arise.

The more important variances may be summarised as:

Materials: price variance and usage variance. Where it is the
practice to fix standard prices for all materials then the
difference between the actual price paid and the standard
price has to be shown. These differences are usually calculated on each purchase invoice and a summary of the invoices
for each month or other period gives the total variance.

Variance in materials usage is the difference between the actual quantity of materials used to produce the quantity of product and the standard quantity. The difference is evaluated at standard prices. In some industries it is relatively simple to calculate the variance but in engineering products of the assembly type this can be very detailed as many components are produced and the variance has to be established for each batch of each component and then a monthly summary prepared. Care has to be taken in doing this that materials attributable to spoilage are segregated.

Operating costs (production). In the chapter dealing with production budgets the treatment of operating costs was centred on particular aspects:

1   *The valuation of productivity.* The standard hours produced by each department were evaluated at the appropriate rates established by the annual budget. This was done in two stages; a rate was fixed for the direct production costs and one for the added costs and a summary prepared under these two headings. It should be noted that where standard costing operates without budgeting much the same procedure has to be followed as in preparing a budget of operating costs as it is necessary to establish rates per standard hour for each department, machine group or cost centre.

2   *Detailed comparison.* The make up of the direct costs was shown against the production value recovered through the standard hours produced. The difference between the production value and the direct costs incurred gave the variance. The same procedure was adopted for added costs. Here the actual costs were detailed under salaries and expenses. This procedure gives a comprehensive and close control of productivity and costs. Budget performance was shown against actual performance to measure the effect on budgeted profit.

3   *The quarterly budget.* This reinforces the procedure mentioned above. The budget covers a period during which the production division has complete control over its operations and it can, therefore, plan on a factual basis and be accountable for its performance. The com-

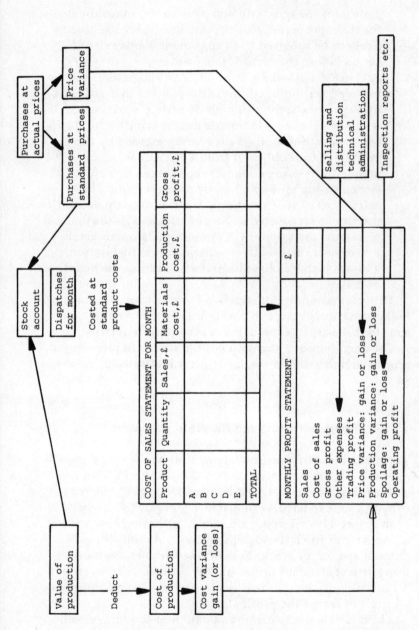

Figure 11.6 Conventional standard costing

parison of the quarterly budget with the annual budget for the same period will indicate in advance the results likely to be achieved and can prompt management action before the event if it is justified.

4   *Spoilage.* In calculating product costs allowances are included for spoilage both with regard to materials and operating costs; the materials by adding a percentage and operating costs by increasing the standard hours. In some industries spoilage may be represented by the yield of output obtained from a given quantity of materials. In engineering it is represented by faulty workmanship as shown by inspection reports. The actual cost of spoilage during a period is compared with the amount recovered in cost of sales and the difference represents the variance. A variance yield can be established more directly by comparing the actual output with what should have been obtained from the quantities of materials used.

The great advantage of standard costs to management is that is can control through exceptions. It reduces the problems to those aspects that are a departure from plan.

The operation of a standard costing system in preparing a profit statement and in valuing stock is illustrated in Figure 11.6.

11.13   Standard costing and the profit statement

The preparation of a profit statement using the conventional standard costing system is illustrated in Figure 11.6. In contrast to this the method used in marginal costing, whereby fixed expenses are excluded, is shown in Figure 11.7.

In Figure 11.6 all values are shown as flowing into and out of stock: into stock through purchases and value of production and out of stock through costs of sales. Purchases go into stock at standard prices and the difference between the actual cost and the standard cost represents the price variance which is shown in the profit statement.

The difference between the valuation of production and the cost of production is the operating costs variance which

Period _____ Month _____ Working days _____

Year to date				PARTICULARS	This period			
Budget		Actual			Budget		Actual	
Amount	%	Amount	%		Amount	%	Amount	%
	100		100	Sales		100		100
				Factory cost of sales:				
				(Variable costs only)				
				Materials cost				
				Production cost				
				TOTAL COST OF SALES				
				Fixed expenses for period				
				TOTAL				
				Factory contribution (gross)				
				Less selling and distribution				
				Less technical				
				Less administration				
				TOTAL				
				Trading profit				
				Price variance: gain or loss				
				Production variance (controllable)				
				Production variance (uncontrollable)				
				Spoilage				
				TOTAL				
				OPERATING PROFIT				

Figure 11.7 Marginal costing system profit statement

is transferred to the profit statement. In productivity costing two variances would be shown, one for productivity and the direct operating costs and one for added costs. The cost of sales statement shows the standard cost for each product and for the quantity sold. A summary of all products gives the sales figure, the total costs of sales and the gross profit which are shown on the profit statement; the cost of sales is deducted from stock.

The gross profit on the profit statement has to be reduced by the operating costs of the other divisions; selling and distribution, technical and administration. The operating costs of the technical division, which includes research, design and development are charged against profit as incurred.

The variances shown on the profit statement have been explained with the exception of spoilage which as previously described is the difference for faulty work included in the cost of sales statement and the actual cost incurred.

All stocks have been shown in a common pool but in practice stock is generally segregated under several headings, for example, stock of raw materials, value of work-in-progress, stock of finished parts and stock of finished products.

11.14   Summary

In the average business with the normal complexities management can only plan effectively through the application of management accounting, first to evaluate the results that can be expected from alternative courses of action and secondly to provide the control information necessary for successful implementation.

Providing cost information as an aid to price-fixing, measuring the profitabilities of different products, providing a yardstick for measuring output, establishing profit/volume relationships — these are some of the more common applications of managing accounting in addition to preparing profit statements and control data. Special investigations for particular purposes are also becoming a regular feature.

It has been seen that an annual budget measures the operating costs of the factory at one level of output only and any deviation from this point invalidates it for controlling costs. The alternative means of controlling costs is through a flexible budget which projects or estimates the costs applicable to varying levels of activity. Another alternative is the short-term budget covering the period during which the factory has full control over its operations. A short-term budget differs from a flexible budget in that it controls productivity as well as costs.

Management accounting is more effective when it can compare actual performance against standard performance and standard costing is valuable for this purpose. Marginal costing has been shown as an alternative to conventional costing. Productivity costing has been mentioned as a means of greater control over productivity and costs. Although based on absorption costing the productivity and direct operating costs could well serve as a substitute for marginal costing.

12 The Profit Budget

The profit budget summarises the information contained in the other budgets and projects the profit expectations for the period under review, usually for the ensuing financial year.

In order to view the profit budget in its proper perspective it is necessary to recapitulate some of the points previously mentioned.

It has to be recognised at the outset that the function and responsibility of management are to exert the maximum influence on the performance of the business and to reflect this in the profit earned. Management has to have a plan of action for the business if profits have to be influenced and not simply left to chance and this plan has to be communicated in clear terms throughout the organisation to ensure effective implementation. The question, therefore, is not whether planning is necessary but how this planning should be done to obtain the best results. The important advantage of budgeting is that it promotes a formalised approach to profit planning. Properly applied it forces management to look at the business and its environment more searchingly and more systematically and from a factual viewpoint.

The annual budget is only one of the constituents of corporate planning but it is important in being the last link in the planning chain that brings to fruition all the plans leading up to it.

Management cannot judge the effect of the annual budget

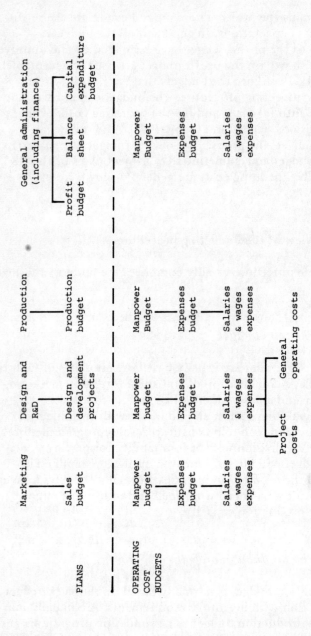

Figure 12.1 Annual budget framework

until it obtains the profit statement and can relate the profit
shown to its expectations. In general if all the budgets
leading up to the profit budget have been studied and approved
the results shown on the profit budget are usually acceptable.

Figure 12.1 outlines the budgets that are normally contained in a budgeting procedure. The budget can normally be
subdivided into (a) plans and (b) the operating costs of the
several divisions. Plans can comprise all of the following:
the sales budget, the production output budget, the materials
purchase budget and, sometimes the project plans of the R&D
division. The operating costs are generally shown for each
division.

12.1   Review of the budgeting procedure

A budgeting procedure usually comprises the undermentioned
budgets.

12.1.1   The sales budget

The prospective sales are usually based on a number of factors,
for example, a combination of statistical forecasts, marketing
intelligence and an assessment of economic conditions.

The annual sales budget should be set with the object of
achievement and it should constitute a sales programme for
the marketing division with accountability for performance.
A sales budget will not be approved until it is examined in
relation to the production facilities; normally the sales budget
has to provide a balanced work load and utilise to a large
extent the production capacity.

12.1.2   The production budget

The production budget is normally based on the sales budget
in conjunction with inventory requirements. A company may
accept the production budget as a production programme and
base its operations accordingly. In this case the performance

and accountability of the production division are measured against the budget.

It is not every company however, probably the minority, that can accept an annual production budget as an operating programme. In these conditions it is advocated that short-term production budgets should be introduced to supplement the annual budget. The period to be covered by the short-term budget depends on the period of time that the production division has complete jurisdiction and control over its operations. Unless the circumstances are exceptional the short-term budget should cover a period of at least three months as any shorter period gives management little opportunity to influence the results. Once a short-term production budget has been approved the production division is accountable for achieving it in terms of both volume and operating costs.

12.1.3   The design and development budget

It is quite usual for companies to direct and control the R&D operations through a series of projects. These projects may be raised in connection with basic research, applied research and a product design and development programme. In some cases the man-hours required for each project are estimated to control the effective use of manpower. In other cases the total cost of the project is estimated and a check is made frequently to compare the actual cost with the estimated cost. It is not unusual to capitalise project costs and write them off over the life of the product. There can be a danger, however, in capitalising project costs because of the unseen difficulties that can arise and which might lead, in effect, to a capitalisation of losses. For this reason the conservative attitude to R&D costs is to write them off against profit within the financial year. In some cases a sum of money is allocated to a project and when the cost incurred reaches this figure the project is considered and a further sum allocated if justified.

12.1.4   Materials purchase budget

Some companies are prepared to place bulk orders for basic
raw materials in accordance with budgeted requirements
even when the annual budget is not acceptable as an operating
programme. The purchase budget is based on an analysis of
the different materials contained in each product multiplied
by the quantity of each product budgeted. Deliveries are
arranged against delivery schedules. The alternative method
of procuring materials is to operate on minimum stock levels
and re-order quantities placing an order as the minimum stock
level is reached. Here there is no necessity, of course, to
prepare a materials purchases budget.

12.1.5   Materials cost budget

Where it is the practice to prepare a materials purchase
budget it is fairly simple to convert it to a materials cost
budget. The prices for the different materials are fixed by
the buying department shortly before the commencement
of the budget year. The object is to estimate the average
price for the ensuing year and to recognise this as the standard
price for costing purposes throughout the year. Differences
between the standard prices and the actual prices paid are
brought out as price variances.

12.1.6   Organisation budget

This is sometimes described as the plan of the organisation or
the manpower budget. The number of persons and the respective grades to be employed in each department or activity are
listed. The salaries and wages payable are calculated at the
appropriate rate for each grade to arrive at a total for the
department. Statutory payments are added to obtain the
payroll budget.

12.1.7   Expenses budget

Any expenditure that is incurred in operating a business,
other than wages and salaries, is generally classed as expenses.

Expenses have to be analysed in a manner to signify the
nature of the expense for identification and control purposes.
It is customary to budget the total for each expense by referring to the cost previously incurred and considering what
increase, if any, is justified. Expenses can be extensive in their
range covering the purchases of indirect materials, purchased
services, such as electricity and telephone, depreciation, taxes,
etc.

An operating cost budget falls under the two headings of
(a) salaries and wages and (b) expenses. Operating cost budgets
have to be prepared for each major division of the business
and subdivided into functions or departments as the circumstances warrant. Budgets have generally to be prepared for the
following divisions: marketing, production, R&D and general
administration.

12.2   Operating costs

It is not unusual to separate the distribution costs from the
general operating costs of the marketing division. The
operating costs of the marketing division may be separated
into salaries and expenses. The salaries may be listed separately
for each function, e.g. selling, sales promotion, market research and sales office, or simply shown as one total. Expenses will probably be listed, e.g. travelling, entertaining,
insurance, depreciation of cars and establishment charges.
The expenses may be allocated to functions to arrive at the
total cost of operating each function. Distribution costs will
show the salaries in total or subdivided by functions or
operations. Expenses may include depots and/or warehouses.
The usual expenses included in distribution are carriage, i.e.
the cost of outside services, the cost of operating company
transport, e.g. depreciation, tax, insurance and running costs
of vehicles and establishment charges.

The operating costs of the marketing division, including
distribution, are written-off in the period on the profit
statement. The operating costs of the production division are
subdivided as previously stated under the two broad headings
of salaries and wages and expenses. There is a further sub-

division into direct operating costs and the indirect operating costs.

The direct operating costs are those that are directly related to the production process as represented by the production departments, or centres; the indirect costs are an aid to production but not a part of it. The indirect costs of production arise from two sources; the indirect costs of the production departments and the cost of operating the indirect departments.

The direct operating costs comprise salaries and wages and expenses. The productive operators are not wholly engaged on productive work because of delays and other interference factors and the wages represented by the hours not on production are classed as indirect labour or, perhaps, labour variance. In some budgeting systems this, indirect labour would not be included in the direct but in the indirect costs. In productivity costing, however, it has to be included in direct costs as it is a factor of productivity.

When dealing with the operating costs of general administration, salaries and wages may be shown in total or subdivided by functions, departments or sections. Expenses are generally itemised. It is quite usual for general administration to include the costs of operating the financial division. The total cost is a charge against profit.

The classification of research, design and development costs are by salaries and wages and expenses. The treatment of R&D costs can vary. Some companies write the operating costs off as incurred. Others tend to capitalise the costs of design projects, writing off only the general costs that are not chargeable against specific projects.

12.3   Accountability for performance

It has been noted that an annual production budget may not be acceptable as a production programme in which case the production division becomes accountable for performance only through a short-term production budget. This compromise is generally confined to the production division. In the case of the sales budget and the other budgets these are action plans that have to be implemented in accordance with the annual budget and involve responsibility and accountability for performance.

12.4 The profit budget

Figure 12.2 shows a profit budget based on the application of productivity costs and added costs as described in detail in the chapter on the production budget; this also shows a quarterly production budget and its application to meet the cases where the annual production budget cannot be applied as a production programme with accountability for performance. The production centre may relate to a department or a group of similar machines.

The steps in preparing the profit budget may be summarised as:

1 *The production output budget.* This is prepared from two sources, an approved sales budget and the inventory plan. The output budget lists the products and the quantity of each to be manufactured in the budget period.

2 *Standard hours.* The standard hours required from each production centre to produce the products in the quantities listed in the output budget are established from the basic records and a summary prepared. The standard hours incorporate an allowance for spoilage. If standard hours cannot be established then production hours can be substituted.

3 *Direct costs of production.* These are summarised under the headings of salaries and wages, labour variance and expenses. The make-up of direct costs has been described in detail in the chapter on the production budget. Labour variance represents idle time or the time spent by the productive operators on non-productive jobs. The salaries and wages of each production centre can be directly charged from the payroll budget. The expenses chargeable to each centre will be allocated on an assessed basis, for example, on floor space in the case of establishment charges.

The direct costs for each centre divided by the stan-

dard hours, or production hours of the centre will give
the rate per standard hour (or production hour).

4   *Added costs.* These include the indirect costs of the
production departments for example, supervision,
clerical and labouring and the costs of operating the
indirect departments such as stores, maintenance, inspection and production planning and control. The
salaries chargeable to each department, production and
indirect, can be ascertained from the payroll budget.
Expenses will be allocated to departments on the bases
of floor space, number of employees in the department,
or other assessment.

The indirect costs of the production departments will
be shown against the respective production centres. The
operating costs of the indirect departments will also be
allocated to the production centres on the basis of an
assessment. The added costs for each production centre
divided by the standard hours for the centre will give a
rate per standard hour for added costs. This procedure
is described in detail in the chapter on the production
budget.

5   *Standard cost of the product.* The production cost of a
product combines the materials cost and the operating
costs of the production division. The operating costs
can be subdivided into direct costs and added costs to
provide more information. The materials cost is ascertained by analysing the various materials and the
quantity that enter into the product costing them at the
standard prices fixed. The standard cost of the product
related to selling price may be shown as in Figure 12.3.

6   *Cost of sales statement.* The budgeted cost of sales
statement starts with the approved sales budget. The
quantity of each product listed is evaluated at the
standard cost of the product. The cost of sales is shown
in Figure 12.2 which also shows the sales extracted from
the sales budget as well as other costs and the gross profit.

7   *The profit statement.* This summarises the information
shown on the cost of sales statement; sales, cost of sales
and gross profit. The budgeted costs of operating the
other divisions, marketing research design and develop-

Year to date		PROFIT STATEMENT	This period	
Budget	Actual	Period	Budget	Actual
		1 Sales		
		Cost of sales:		
		2 Materials cost		
		3 Direct operating costs		
		4 Added costs		
		5 TOTAL		
		6 GROSS PROFIT (1 – 5)		
		Other costs:		
		7 Marketing		
		8 Research and development		
		9 General administration		
		TOTAL		
		10 Trading profit		
		11 Variances (gain or loss)		
		Materials prices		
		Materials usage		
		Direct operating costs		
		Added costs		
		Spoilage		
		TOTAL		
		12 NET OPERATING PROFIT		
		Quarterly budget. Variances		
		Direct operating costs		
		Added costs		

Figure 12.2 Annual budget profit statement

ment and general administration, are then deducted to show the net profit before tax. This presumes that the costs of operating the R&D function are written off in the year that these are incurred.

8   *Quarterly production budget.* This budget is only necessary when the annual production budget cannot be accepted as a production programme. In preparing the quarterly budget the production division must be guided by the facts of the situation and not influenced by the annual budget. The information that has to be provided is:

a   The standard hours required from each production centre.

b   The salaries and wages payable to the production centres in total. There is no need to analyse these by production centres.

c   The expenses to be included in the direct operating costs. Each expense is shown in total as again there is no need to analyse by departments. Some of the expenses listed may be common to the indirect departments and then the amount of the expense has to be apportioned between the direct costs and the indirect costs.

d   The salaries and wages to be paid to the indirect workers in the production centres and to the indirect departments. These are shown in total only and not analysed by departments.

e   The expenses to be incurred as indirect costs in the production centres and the indirect departments. It may be necessary to apportion some expenses between direct costs and indirect costs. This apportionment is done in total only and not by departments.

An example of a quarterly budget was given in the chapter on the production budget. The points to be particularly noted are:

f   The standard hours for each production centre are evaluated at the rate per standard hour fixed by the *annual budget* to obtain the total value of production. This total is then compared with the

	£	£
Selling price		x
Less Materials cost	x	
Less Direct operating costs	x	x
BALANCE: Contribution		x
Less Added costs		x
Gross profits		x

Figure 12.3   Standard cost of product related to selling price

total direct costs shown on the quarterly budget and the variance established.

g   The same process is repeated for added costs by evaluating the standard hours at the rate fixed by the annual budget for each production centre. The total allowance for added costs compared with the the total shown on the quarterly budget for added costs gives the variance.

h   The quarterly budget is compared with the annual budget for the same period, i.e. for the same number of working days. This is done to obtain a comparison in detail. The annual budget obviously shows no variances.

In formulating a budgeting procedure it is essential to provide the basis for controlling performance against budget. There are many ways of doing this dependent upon the product and the method of manufacture.

12.5   Comparison of actual and budgeted performance

In general there are two systems of costing that can be effectively applied dependent upon the product and the volume of manufacture. There is the output costing system where the nature of production is such that output can measure productivity. A typical example is the manufacture of a particular chemical using production facilities that are specifically designed for the product. An example of this application was given in an earlier chapter.

The alternative is productivity costing which is applied when output does not measure productivity. Here a synthetic unit instead of a natural unit of output has to be applied to measure productivity. This alternative has by force of circumstances a fairly extensive application. In the manufacture of engineering products of the assembly type productivity has generally to be measured through synthetic units and the one most frequently adopted is the standard hour which is a unit of work as defined by work study.

Productivity costing has been discussed in detail and it is only necessary at this point to consider the main essentials.

The first point to be noted is that the annual budget establishes two cost rates per standard hour for each production centre, one for the direct operating costs associated with productivity and the other for the indirect costs termed added costs.

In comparing actual performance with budgeted performance the procedure is:

1 To summarise the standard hours produced in the month, or four weeks, by each production centre and evaluate them at the appropriate standard hourly rate budgeted for the centre in respect of direct costs. A summary of these figures for all production centres will provide the value of production.
2 To establish the direct costs incurred during the same period. This will be shown in total and not by production centres.
3 The difference between the production value and the direct costs incurred will give the variance. This variance will represent the amount gained or loss and will also measure productivity.
4 Added costs will be dealt with in a similar manner and the amount allowed through the standard hours produced at the appropriate hourly rates budgeted for each centre will be compared with the total added costs actually incurred and the variance, favourable or unfavourable, established.

It is important to note that variances are not established by taking the difference between actual figures and budgeted figures as is common in many costing systems. The actual figures for the period provide the variances. In preparing a quarterly or short term production budget the budgeted

standard hours for each production centre are evaluated at
the standard hourly rates established by the annual budget.
As example of a quarterly budget was given in the chapter
on the production budget.

The profit and loss statement shown in Figure 12.2 presents
the sort of comparison that can be made between actual and
budgeted performance. This statement shows the actual
figures for the month compared with the budget and the
cumulative figures for the year to date. The budget figures
for any month are based on the number of working days in
the month so that the actual figures and the budget are on a
comparable basis.

The sales are obtained from a summary of the sales invoices. The cost of sales are derived from the standard costs
of the products and the quantities sold. The sales less cost of
sales show the gross profit. The costs of operating the other
divisions have to be deducted to arrive at the trading profit.
This presumes that the costs of operating these divisions will
be charged as incurred each month.

Variances have been discussed previously and will only be
described briefly at this point. Price variance is the difference
between the standard priced fixed at the commencement of
the financial year and the actual prices paid. The figure is
obtained from an analysis of purchase invoices. The materials
usage variance can generally be established in one of two
ways: (a) by calculating the standard materials cost for the
output obtained and comparing with the actual cost, or (b)
by calculating the output that should have been obtained
from the materials used and comparing this with the actual
output.

The variances in direct operating costs and added costs are
calculated from the performance statements of the production
division. Figures 9.10 and 9.11 illustrated the procedure. It is
not sufficient, however, to state what the variances are without any qualifying remark. This is where the short-term
budget plays an important part. In discussing the production
budget a statement was shown comparing the quarterly budget with the corresponding period of the annual budget. The
variances shown were considered to be uncontrollable against
a quarterly budget. These variances for the quarter are

translated into monthly variances in proportion to the working days in each month. The variances are recorded at the foot of the profit statement to indicate the extent that the variances in the body of the profit statement are uncontrollable.

Spoilage is usually ascertained from inspection reports which provide the information necessary to establish the cost figures. Frequently a spoilage allowance is included in the standard cost of the product. The spoilage figure to be shown on the profit statement is, therefore, the difference between the cost of spoilage for the month and the amount allowed for spoilage in the cost of sales for the month. The total of the variances are added or deducted from the trading profit, according to being favourable or unfavourable, to arrive at the operating profit.

12.6   Balance sheet

It is an accepted principle in a sound budgeting scheme that the financial position should be shown at the beginning of the budget period together with a projection of the position at the end of the period.

This kind of comparison can run into great detail and here only the salient points will be considered. The statement usually starts with the budgeted profit for the year. The tax assessment is deducted to arrive at the profit after tax. Appropriations of profit, dividends etc. are deducted to establish the undistributed profit. Depreciation is added back to this figure.

The next stage is to consider the movements that will take place in the current assets and liabilities (see Figure 12.4). In addition to change in current assets and liabilities there is always the question of capital expenditure to be taken into account and funds have to be available to meet it.

Where a company is increasing its sales it usually follows that debtors increase and also the inventory. This output may be offset by adding back depreciation and taking account of undistributed profit and a reasonable increase in trade creditors. Where those increases in current assets plus capital

	Increase	Decrease
Current Assets	£	£
Bank balance		
Trade debtors		
Inventory		
Investments		
Other debtors		
Total		
Current Liabilities		
Trade creditors		
Other creditors		
Bank overdraft		
Loans		
Total		

Figure 12.4   Movements in current assets and liabilities

expenditure cannot be offset in the manner indicated then the company may draw on its investments, if it has any, or increase its bank overdraft. If these measures are not sufficient the company may consider an increase in share capital or arrange special loans if its profit record warrants them.

The progressive company has to be alive to the dangers of overtrading to the point where its growth cannot be supported financially. The advantage of a financial budget is that it projects the likely conditions ahead of events and permits a company to prepare for them or to adjust its plans.

The key factors in preparing a financial budget are the profit budget, the capital expenditure budget and the balance sheet. The balance sheet is generally regarded as the financial budget but some companies prefer to create a separate budget to regulate and control the availability of funds.

12.7   The art of budgeting

Sophisticated management is the most essential factor in the art of budgeting. It has to be recognised that budgeting is not only a function of management but one of the more important processes of management. Top management involvement is essential for success. While much of the work must be delegated to divisional managers and the like it must be delegation with proper control.

The principles and practices developed and proven over the years by many of the leading companies of America and Europe should be known and applied as the direct route to the art of budgeting.

There has to be a factual approach to budgeting. Management must decide what information it requires to make the decisions involved. It must be prepared to go to great lengths to establish the facts. The final act in decision making is to exercise judgement on all the facts that can be made available.

A budget must be determined with a view to implementation. Budgeting must be used as an instrument of management control through built-in procedures that monitor performance against budget. Budgets must impose personal responsibilities with accountability for performance. Budgets are frequently described as 'estimates'. But they must be estimates in the proper sense with every possible step taken to ensure their accuracy. They must be 'statements of probabilities'. Unless this standard is attained the value of budgets as a means of projecting probable results and monitoring performance will be seriously impaired and accountability and performance weakened.

It has to be appreciated that an annual budget has largely to accept the conditions as they are and make the most of them. Creating the right conditions for profitable operation is generally a long-term consideration that is embraced by strategic planning. The facts behind the figures of the annual profit and loss statements of most successful companies will generally show that their success is attributable to decisions made and action taken three or four years previously. The fact is that a year is a short period in the profit span of most companies.

In general annual budgeting can influence the profit but it cannot create the conditions fundamental to it.

12.8   Summary

A profit budget can take many forms as can the other budgets that it comprises. A comprehensive knowledge of the principles with illustrations of their application can be invaluable but in the end the system to be applied must be tailor-made to the requirements of the particular business.

It has to be recognised that budgeting like all the other constituents of corporate planning is not simply a tool of management but is an important function of management. Budgets simply reflect the management plans in financial terms and in general will be no better or no worse than the plans themselves. It can be said for budgeting, however, that it makes management think and plan more systematically and to greater purpose and in those respects alone it makes a worthwhile contribution.

Index